ETHEREUM FOR BUSINESS

Ethereum for Business

A Plain-English Guide to the Use Cases
that Generate Returns from Asset
Management to Payments to Supply Chains

Paul Brody

epic.
books

Fayetteville
2023

Library of Congress Control Number: 2023939466

ISBN: 978-1-954892-10-1
eISBN: 978-1-954892-11-8

27 26 25 24 23   5 4 3 2 1

∞ The paper used in this publication meets the minimum requirements of
the American National Standard for Permanence of Paper for Printed Library
Materials Z39.48-1984.

Cover by Notch Design
Illustrations by LogicBeach.eth
Edited by Ben Schiller

Cataloging-in-Publication Data on file at the Library of Congress.

Contents

Foreword

Over the decade in which I've been observed the blockchain industry's many twists, turns, booms and busts, we've witnessed two competing strains of development.

One was founded entirely on native, on-chain tokens and transactions and so-called public, or permissionless blockchains such as Ethereum. With its roots in the breakthrough Bitcoin idea that money can be an entirely digital artifact, it has focused on the online environment as its own, enclosed economy. The other strain dealt with the analog world. It sought to apply smart contracts, data-tracking and other aspects of blockchain technology to the problems of existing businesses and communities.

The first, which over time attracted the moniker of "crypto," faced scaling challenges – as much a governance obstacle as a technological one, since the very nature of decentralized networks makes it difficult and time-consuming to find acceptable consensus around upgrades. It also ran into privacy risks, with the public structure of permissionless blockchains making it hard to protect both individuals' personal data and business secrets. And then there were the security and UX issues as wallets were relentlessly hacked and as the processes used to guard against those threats made the experience prohibitively complicated for mass adoption.

The second field of blockchain development emerged during the "Crypto Winter" of 2014-2015, which took hold after the collapse in the Mt. Gox exchange popped the bitcoin bubble of 2013. With several bankers and industrialists encouraging people to embrace "blockchain, not bitcoin," the idea of "enterprise blockchain" was born. But it also struggled – for different reasons that can essentially be boiled down to the fact that, in trying to solve for public blockchains' limitations, these early enterprise solutions stripped the technology of its real purpose.

Most of the early business-focused solutions were built on permissioned blockchains. Businesses, understandably wary of revealing sensitive information to partners and competitors, were uncomfortable ceding control to an amorphous community of developers, crypto miners and traders. So, they put a centralized authority in charge – sometimes a consortium of business partners, other times a single company – to decide who could participate in the network. To many in the crypto world, this was absurd. The whole idea behind Bitcoin and Ethereum was that they offered an open-source, permissionless environment in which anyone could run a node, anyone could own the tokens and anyone could build other products and applications on top of the protocol. Not having to trust a gatekeeper was the technology's power, not its weakness.

As it turns out, the crypto critics proved prophetic. Many of these enterprise blockchains folded for the predictable reason that outside partners and competitors were unwilling to help build a network of shared information that was controlled by IBM, or by Maersk, or by Walmart or by a consortium of Wall Street banks.

What unfolded was an interesting cycle in which the limitations of crypto would shift attention to enterprise blockchain until the latter's failures were overshadowed by some new exciting innovation emerging out of the former's open-source community – be it initial coin offerings (ICOs), non-fungible tokens (NFTs) or decentralized finance (DeFi.) At those times, crypto would attract a frenzy of speculation and, ultimately, a market bubble would grow until it burst, the implosion typically triggered by a regulatory crackdown or by the exposure of a major scam or failure. Then the next phase of the cycle, a return to the real economy of enterprise blockchain ideas, would begin.

We are currently in that phase, one of renewed interest in enterprise blockchain ideas. After the massive losses from the collapse of FTX and the evaporation of confidence in the crypto industry, along with U.S. regulators' crackdown on token exchanges, the conversation has turned to ensuring that investor returns are based on delivering real utility to people and businesses rather than on the circular logic of "number go up" speculation. The talk now is of tokenizing "real-world assets," of Web3 loyalty programs for major consumer brands and of tackling climate change with carbon-tracking blockchain applications.

Is this latest phase doomed to fail like the previous enterprise blockchain moment?

As an observer of markets and human behavior whose profession is founded on skepticism, I always hesitate to say "this time is different." Still, I see a trend that makes this current moment special, one that challenges the simplistic idea encouraged in my preceding paragraphs that these two strains of blockchain development are necessarily in natural competition with each other. It's a trend driven by the quiet but relentless force of cryptographic innovation, which has reached a point where these two fields can merge. New "Layer 2" and zero-knowledge-proof inventions are poised to solve the scaling, privacy and security challenges that have dogged public blockchain platforms at the same time that visionary developers of enterprise solutions such as Paul Brody – who has always understood the power of "permissionlessness" – are figuring out how to apply them to business use cases.

Here is the hopeful core message of Brody's invaluable book: we are entering a best-of-both-worlds scenario in which crypto's inventive use of tokenization and decentralized information-sharing can now finally be safely applied to businesses. Judging by the many exciting use cases he cites – highlighted with numerous on-the-ground projects in varying stages of development, including those of EY clients such Casa Girelli Wines, Peroni Beer, Microsoft and Takeda Pharmaceuticals – this "cryptofication" of enterprise blockchain will have a profound impact on the global economy.

Brody's belief is that this process will play out much like most technology revolutions by defaulting to a single, preferred standard for the entire world. In his view, that standard is defined by the Ethereum blockchain and the ecosystem of associated protocols built on and around it. Unlike many prior technological waves, however, this one should not drive us into the capture of corporate middlemen since Ethereum is not governed by a single corporate entity. It's closer to the open internet standards of TCP/IP, HTTP, SMTP and so forth. Yes, it means early holders of Ether are destined to get even more fabulously rich, but in theory they shouldn't be able to control users' lives in the way that, say, Apples does with its IOS platform or Google does with it search algorithm, browser and geospatial technologies.

I personally am not ready to conclude that the public blockchain founded by Vitalik Buterin will definitely be The One, but Brody makes a compelling argument that network effects and the collective power of developer activity are strongly in its favor. If he's right, that's not great news for all the competing "Layer 1" protocols but it will favor the interoperability and efficiencies that are needed if blockchain technology is to live up to its potential to transform the global economy.

Whether Brody is right that Ethereum is the winner, or whether the prize ends up going to another Layer 1 or perhaps to an interoperability protocol that enables many blockchains to seamlessly coexist, the power of this book is that it reveals a world of possibilities in a new, open innovation era of enterprise blockchain development. It's a roadmap for building a business in the soon-to-be decentralized age.

Michael J. Casey

Chief Content Officer, CoinDesk

Co-author, *The Age of Cryptocurrency: How Bitcoin and Digital Money Are Challenging the Global Economic Order* and *The Truth Machine: The Blockchain and the Future of Everything*

I.

AN OVERVIEW OF ETHEREUM

CHAPTER 1

About This Book

How To Read This Book

Early on, when I told my friends I was writing a book, I said it was a romance novel. That wasn't true, but it also wasn't a lie. I love what I do and I have approached my work on Ethereum as a bit of a mission.

You can read this book from start to finish and it should be quite "readable." I don't know if you'll cry at the end, though I'm doing everything in my power to create a happy ending. If you are not familiar with blockchain, this book is designed to be read in a linear fashion, one chapter building on the next. I go into the basics of blockchain technology and key components like wallets, tokens, and keys, then on to the use cases. I finish up with some of the advanced topics that often come up as people learn about this technology, including carbon footprints, audits, and security.

You can also read this book by dipping in and out of chapters. Each one, especially the chapters on business use cases or key technology components like tokenization or privacy, are designed to be stand-alone. Throughout, I do my best to minimize jargon and use plain English.

I have tried to avoid too many references to other chapters in the book. I'm already deeply traumatized on this issue by a Thomas Keller cookbook that had so many internal references that a simple recipe turned into a day-long cooking marathon that left me exhausted and emotionally wrecked.

I also apologize for my sense of humor.

Who Should Read This Book

When I wrote this book, I had two audiences in mind. The first is business executives who want to understand the fuss about blockchain and want to see if it can actually be useful in solving real-world business problems.

The second audience is people who know more about blockchains, especially on the technical side, and want to get a perspective on the business use cases. The world of blockchain has done a great deal of work in areas like financial services, but not much on industrial applications, for example in tokenization and supply chains.

Please forgive all technical simplifications. I've done my best to have very clever people read them and point out errors, but I've also avoided some of the subtle detail involved that more experienced users will already understand.

This is an Ethereum Book. This isn't an EY Book

My day job is being the Global Blockchain Leader at EY (Ernst & Young), and it's a job I love very much because it has given me the opportunity to make big contributions to the Ethereum ecosystem and build a great business inside a world-leading professional services partnership. That being said, this book is a personal project for me and, to the extent that it's possible, I've tried to separate my day-job from my hobbies. I hope you won't come away from this book thinking that it was just a big advertisement for EY. It's not meant to be.

In the interest of transparency, I have shared the draft of the book with my colleagues at EY for their comments and so they're not surprised by the inclusion of a case study about an EY client.

Additionally, to avoid even the appearance of a conflict of interest, I have committed to donate all profits from the book to fund public goods through Gitcoin, which is led by incredible people dedicated to making the world a better place (and is also a case study of a DAO in the book).

While it's not intended as an ad for EY, this book is an advertisement for Ethereum. I very consciously chose the title for this book because it's not just about any blockchain or blockchains in general. I take a whole chapter to explain why I think Ethereum is the winner in the standards war and why blockchains, like a lot of digital systems, are natural monopolies.

I'm deeply engaged in the Ethereum community and I am also a member of the board of directors of the Ethereum Enterprise Association (EEA) and I tend to participate in a lot of official and unofficial Ethereum events and activities. All of which is to say that on this particular topic, I'm very much not objective or unbiased.

Case Studies in This Book

This book contains a number of case studies and examples. Some of these are from EY work and some are not. Nearly all are from the world of Ethereum. I've reached out to each company discussed here and asked for their review of my notes, though in a few cases either I didn't receive a reply or the firm is no longer around to review my draft. Though I did receive help from the EY account teams and project teams updating and documenting case studies of EY work and EY clients, no non-public information is included here unless it was specifically approved by the company for release.

- AAVE
- ANSA
- Casa Girelli Wines, Italy
- Circle
- Coinbase
- ContourNetwork
- CryptoPunks
- Digital Naira
- Digital Yuan (DCEP)
- Fireblocks
- GitCoin
- IBM Food Trust
- United Nations International Fund for Agricultural Development (IFAD)
- International Monetary Fund
- MakerDAO
- Mediledger
- Microsoft
- Chainlink
- Peroni Beer
- Stasis Euro
- Takeda Pharmaceuticals
- TradeLens
- Uniswap

Subject Matter Experts

In addition to the cooperation and review of many companies, I need to thank a number of subject matter experts inside and outside of EY who have so kindly assisted in reviewing, editing, commenting and giving interviews to support the creation of this book.

- Pano Anthos. Founder and Managing Director, XRC Ventures
- Vitalik Buterin, Ethereum Foundation
- James Canterbury, Partner, EY
- Michael Casey, Chief Content Officer, CoinDesk
- Horace Dediu, Founder/Author, Asymco.com

- Federico Di Poli, Product Manager, OpsChain, EY
- Matthew Foster, PhD Candidate, Pepperdine University
- Tom Garlick, Senior Manager, EY
- Pramodh Gopalakrishna, Senior Manager, EY
- Matthew Hatch, Partner, EY
- Arwin Holmes, Senior Manager, EY
- Richard Hueskin, Partner, EY
- Prof Mary Lacity, Director, Blockchain Center of Excellence, Sam M Walton College of Business, University of Arkansas
- Mark MacDonald, Partner, EY
- Gaeron McClure, Partner, EY
- Igor Mikhailev, Partner, EY
- JT Nichol, r/EthFinance
- Giuseppe Perrone, Partner, EY Blockchain
- Rodney Ramcharan, Professor of Finance, University of Southern California
- Amarjit Singh, Partner, EY
- Ryan Sheets, EPIC Books, University of Arkansas
- Carl Wegner, CEO, Countour.Network
- Kyle Weiss, Chief Operating Officer, Gitcoin DAO
- Duncan Westland, Director, EY
- Jeff Wong, Partner & Chief Innovation Officer, EY
- Chen Zur, Partner, EY Blockchain

CHAPTER 2

My Introduction to Ethereum

There are many books about the origins of Ethereum, so I'm not going to attempt to re-hash that history here. What I am going to tell you about is how I came to see Ethereum as an essential piece of business infrastructure.

My background is in a combination of business strategy, with a couple of years at McKinsey & Co., and a lot of time in business operations, primarily in supply chain planning. While I started my career in strategy, I quickly moved on to the work of execution and in particular, to the problem of how to scale up execution using technology.

After McKinsey I went to i2 Technologies, one of the early pioneers in constraint-based business planning and later to ClearCross, a specialist in cross-border logistics. ClearCross folded in 2001, a victim of too much venture capital and not enough management spending restraint, and then joined my friend Ruby Sahiwal in a procurement analytics start-up called Aentropy.

After bouncing around the world of start-ups for a while, I realized that I was probably not going to start my own company and, if I wanted to become a CEO, the only other path was to be brought in as adult supervision. Fast growing companies seemed to be in the practice of hiring outside CEOs from big established firms to fill that role. Those firms include companies like IBM, so in 2002 as Aentropy was sold off, I took a position at IBM in the supply chain strategy and consulting organization.

I spent the next thirteen years at IBM, with about a nine-month detour to co-found my own company. (Because, of course, that's what happens when you try to predict your own future and you're certain you'll never be a founder.) We crashed and burned and I returned to IBM, this time as the Vice President for the electronics industry.

Of all the jobs I had prior to leading blockchain at EY, this was by far the most enjoyable. Working with an industry sector that encompassed everything from medical devices to TVs to appliances turned out to be amazing for someone who loves learning about process. Over the years, I've gotten to see everything from aircraft production lines to the inside of a nuclear reactor (not yet fueled!). I've donned bunny suits, hard-hats, and ear protection in just about every kind of manufacturing and logistics operation in most corners of the planet. It's endlessly interesting to me and I consider myself to be astonishingly lucky to have found such a job.

Perhaps the perk I enjoyed most while working in this job was the access I got to IBM's brilliant research staff. There was an expectation that industry VPs should produce at least one piece of original insight and vision each year, looking at key issues for their industry. In 2012, I made a deep dive into 3D printing, which included buying a washing machine, taking it apart, scanning each individual piece in 3D and then attempting to re-build the thing using a 3D printer. It was immense fun – and that includes explaining to IBM procurement why I needed them to approve the purchase of a washing machine.

A Tale of Two Chips

As 2013 rolled around, I was noodling on what to do next when I became aware of a number of different pieces of data that suggested how complex smart device networks could or should be built. The first came from a visit to a major U.S. appliance manufacturer.

Making appliances is often talked about in the context of hammering big pieces of metal into different shapes and sticking a motor on them, and there's some truth to that, but increasingly, in the 2010s, companies were concerned with making their devices smart.

There was a lot of discussion at the time, still going on to this day, about what kind of smarts these devices should have. The ability to start the oven remotely seems like a great way to burn your house down. Nor is it practical to leave a roast sitting at room temperature in your oven all day until 5pm and switch it on remotely. I'm no expert on food safety but this doesn't seem like a good idea either. On the other hand, recipes saying things like "bake until golden brown" are frustrating to me. I don't want to sit by the oven looking in every two minutes, so a video camera that can detect what golden brown looks like, shutting off the oven accordingly while notifying you, would be cool.

I started, at that point, an unsuccessful campaign to get my IBM colleagues to build a toaster with imaging software in it and show the world how to make a perfect piece of toast. I thought it would be a fun demonstration of how you make a truly useful smart device, complete with IoT software and management infrastructure. I've always loved these kinds of hybrid theory and reality projects. And I needed a new toaster at home. Why not have IBM spend a couple million dollars to get one that really works well?

While I was contemplating these questions and lobbying to build a multi-million-dollar prototype toaster, I got hit with three interesting problems by clients:

1. **Appliance chips aren't nearly smart enough**. Typical "white goods" like refrigerators or washing machines, use an embedded processor that is designed to be inexpensive to mass produced and low-cost. These typically run $5-10 at scale and take a significant time to prepare and design. They're not very "bright," but they can manage basic functions like keeping the light on when the door opens and regulating temperature. What there isn't, in these systems, is the capacity to significantly add functions like remote management, video, or other services.

2. **Smartphone chips are getting absurdly cheap**. At the same time that appliance chips are not smart enough, the cost of really smart chips, the ones that power smartphones, is coming down. At scale, these computer-on-a-chip devices cost as little as $5. They were, as far back as 2013, becoming ubiquitous and cheap. So much so that even very smart cables had them embedded inside the cable. The anecdote which blew my mind was hearing about how Apple's own Lightning Digital AV adapter had an ARM SOC that booted MacOS when plugged in and ran a software-based real-time video conversion tool.

3. **Device management costs are a poorly controlled expense at big companies.** Much of the "smart" in smart-devices depends upon centralized servers. When you buy a $1,000 phone or tablet, the attached "free" cloud computing services are handy and can cost $10/user/year. That's a manageable cost when you've spent $1,000 and are going to buy a new one in three to three years. But what happens if you buy a smart, connected light-bulb or radio that doesn't come with 30-40% gross margins? And what if the expected life of that product isn't 2-3 years, but 10 to 20? Now you have an emerging cost-containment problem.

This last problem was put to me in 2013 by TJ Kang, who, at the time, was the SVP in charge of Samsung's multi-media solution center (MSC). As TJ pointed out, Samsung was starting to anticipate not millions but billions of connected devices. What was a small problem at the time would or could morph into a financial black hole if left unaddressed.

As I started to absorb all these different data-points in 2013, I had a couple of "aha" moments. The first was that intelligence will be ubiquitous in the future because intelligence is becoming, in effect, free. If an embedded control chip costs you $5 and does only minimal work, and a smartphone System-on-a-Chip (SoC) also costs $5, why not put in a programmable, adaptable, smart device? It's cheaper and more flexible. Intelligence, I realized, now has a marginal additional cost of near-zero.

The second "aha" moment was that if people start putting very smart chips on devices everywhere, then there should be less of a need for all that costly cloud computing infrastructure. Imagine a million washing machines with smartphone chips in them, connected to electrical power and WiFi. What are they doing 99% of the time? NOTHING. If Apple can put an entire Mac with 2GB of RAM in an HDMI cable, then surely all these smart, connected appliances can, collectively, form some kind of distributed cloud. Why shouldn't the washing machines of the world back each other up and operate as a distributed cloud? The cloud, as the T-shirt says, is just someone else's computer.

And so, ADEPT was born. ADEPT stands for Autonomous Decentralized Peer-to-peer Telemetry. It was intended as a prototype of a distributed computing network that could be installed on smart devices and they would be able to start managing and operating as a decentralized cloud. The vision was that, eventually, companies like Samsung could reduce their cloud computing footprint for smart devices by up to 99%, just keeping a kind of centralized tab on the whole ecosystem. TJ Kang at Samsung bravely volunteered to work with us on the prototype and put it into some Samsung devices as a test.

Distributed Computing Meet Blockchain

There are, in fact, many different distributed computing systems out there. Distributed computing is not a new idea, but it's "high overhead" and hasn't gained a lot of traction. What was different in 2013 and still is different today is that thanks to Moore's Law, there's a lot of idle computing power out there. In fact, there are several orders of magnitude more computing power in the world's pockets and on desks in cars than there is in all the world's data centers.

And most of the time, it's not doing much at all. So even if distributed computing isn't particularly efficient, it doesn't matter if all that computing power has little else to do anyway. And so I waved goodbye to my dreams of a very smart toaster and we assembled a team from IBM Research, the electronics industry business unit, and Samsung to get going on a distributing cloud model for IoT devices.

From the beginning, we started to get interested in blockchain. Our initial look was at Bitcoin. We liked the idea of identities, accounts, and payments. Eventually, if this distributed cloud thing got big enough, people would be buying and selling computing services on this network, we thought. Each device might be entitled to infinitesimally small payments for its computing power, covering the cost of incremental power and bandwidth needed. In practice, Bitcoin seemed a bit slow. We joked that the last thing you wanted was to stand outside in the rain for 10 minutes while a block completed and you waited for your smartwatch to unlock your front door.

Not long into the project, John Cohn, one of IBM's most distinguished engineers, came to me with an idea. What about Ethereum? He had met some people involved in the alpha version of Ethereum, specifically, Vitalik Buterin. Vitalik believed in the technical vision of Bitcoin but wanted to apply it to generalized computing challenges rather than just payments. It was appealing. It didn't solve all our problems, but it seemed to work much more closely in alignment with our goals. You could build and run actual applications with Solidity code and it had the core account and payment features of Bitcoin. It became a longstanding joke in our team: we didn't know what people would pay for in the world of Internet of Things (IoT). But we were sure that someone would pay for something and we'd need accounts and smart contracts for that.

So, in the end, we went with the alpha version of Ethereum. To that, we added some additional features. We wanted quick communications, so we included the messaging protocol Telehash, and we wanted to enable large data downloads without clogging up the chain. So we integrated BitTorrent, all with significant amounts of help from Vitalik Buterin and some of the other early Ethereum volunteers.

The result was, at least in theory, an integrated distributed cloud infrastructure that could be used to manage large scale IoT device networks. We then squeezed the whole thing down to fit on a couple of Samsung appliances and showed the result off in January 2015 at the Consumer Electronics Show in Las Vegas. It was an immensely exciting moment for me and, to this day, I remain deeply disappointed that it was never turned into a full scale product or deployed. I haven't lost hope for this part of the blockchain ecosystem, but I have accepted that perhaps we were just too early in our vision.

From IoT to Everything

I was, to say the least, smitten with this idea of distributed computing and blockchains. The more I learned about Ethereum and blockchains, the more certain I became that this technology would come to have a profound impact on the world of business.

In particular, I believe that Ethereum can and will solve a fundamental problem that plagues modern enterprises: data quality. I have learned, over the years, that nothing is more scarce than good data. From strategy work to business forecasting, we have an abundance of tools that are good at planning.

From strategic planning to inventory management, there are good algorithms and frameworks available, but they're close to useless without accurate data.

In banks, data is like money. It is, in fact, pretty much the same as money. So banks put a lot of effort into keeping track of money. Very, very tightly. Large companies and their inventories: not so much, even though inventory is, really, just another form of money. In the world of banking, when you want to put money in one account, you need to take it from another. There are very strict controls on who can "create" money.

In the world of industry, the same controls are not in place. I can "create" inventory just about anywhere I want. Just because I am receiving something from a supplier doesn't mean they deducted that inventory from their systems. Now, that doesn't mean they don't try and it doesn't mean that companies don't put a lot of effort into tracking their assets, but they lack the discipline and rigor of inter-bank or intra-bank payments.

The result is a gradual decay of information quality as stuff and data move through the global economy. Much of what we think is "good forecasting" and "accurate data" is really just the good fortune that this year's data looks pretty much like last year. Even though I have been deeply involved in the world of supply chain planning for many years, I never realized how much we depend upon these predictable patterns until the COVID pandemic. The sudden shift from services (going out) to products (staying in at home) exposed how poorly prepared supply chains were for real changes.

With tokenization on Ethereum, I started to see a way to apply the discipline of banking to the world of supply chain and business operations. Instead of creating and deleting data as products and services move between firms, we can create tokens that can be moved between firms, treated like money with end to end reconciliation, and these items would have continuity of existence on Ethereum. Entire supply chains and business ecosystems could be digitized.

In 2014, my colleagues at IBM came to see blockchain as an interesting distraction at best and a threat to the server business at worst. I was asked to wrap up my work in blockchain and move on, but I didn't want to. By the end of 2014, it was clear that if I wanted to pursue blockchain seriously, I'd have to change firms, so I did.

Once I joined EY, I started the serious work involved in getting the organization to take blockchain seriously and treat it not just as an interesting technology, but as a truly transformational one. But that's a story for another day.

More Efficiency, Fewer Monopolies

If there's one other thing I want to touch on in relating my trip down the rabbit hole into the world of Ethereum, it's my interest in making this technology work for the public and the world, not just for enterprises. Already in my time at IBM, it was becoming clear that digital marketplaces inexorably result in digital monopolies.

The economics of software and digital networks drive the world towards monopolies. Software has its own special form of economics: the marginal cost of a new user is, effectively, at or near zero. Once you have built a solid user base and paid off your initial development costs, you can afford to see off the competition by continuously lowering the price of renewals and updates and extensions. You make money at any price above zero.

Digital networks have a similar kind of effect. Metcalf's Law, which says that the value of a network is equal to the square of the number of users, doesn't just apply to simple data networks like Ethernet or the Internet. It applies to just about any kind of business where there are network effects. A digital network with more customers is more attractive to sellers and the more sellers that join, the more customers are attracted. At a certain point, it becomes exceptionally hard for competing digital markets to take off.

When you combine these two effects, you get the recipe for a new era of digital monopolies. From online auctions to ride sharing to vacation apartment rental, you have business ecosystems that are built on software and have powerful network effects. The result is a gradual path towards a single firm dominating these markets.

Don't get me wrong. At first, these networks like auctions, ride-sharing, and more create enormous value for customers. The software and tools developed enable a complex multi-party transaction to take place, coordinating, product or service selection, delivery and payment. I remember getting out of a ride-share the first time and just walking away. It was like magic compared to the fumbling that goes on in a taxi at the end of ride.

Eventually, however, digital markets shift from connecting buyers and sellers and creating value to extracting value from all the participants. Once a monopoly or near monopoly situation looks stable, the central network operators always start tweaking fees and operating models that maximize their profits, not ecosystem value creation as a whole.

Businesses have been fairly careful about embracing digital transaction networks because of fears of this effect. Consumers have gone first and companies have seen what happens from operating systems to ride sharing. But what if there was a mechanism to have all the benefits of digital collaboration without the monopoly risk? Then they might embrace and accelerate their digital transformation.

Already in 2013 and 2014, as I was writing the IBM white paper on using blockchains for IoT networks a somewhat utopian strain of thinking was already starting to permeate my thinking. It's no accident we called our original paper on the topic "Device Democracy" because we saw the transformation power of blockchains to decentralized device control. (Both that paper and the follow-on I helped author, The Economy of Things," are still available from the IBM web site to download.)

That is the opportunity I see in Ethereum for enterprises (and for consumers as well). Ethereum, like the Internet, can become a kind of monopoly. But if it's a decentralized monopoly with no controlling entity to start extracting value, it can be one that creates value for everyone and then returns the value to those who are working in the system.

I hope, as you read this book, you'll come to see how valuable Ethereum can be to your business. If you happen to make our global economy more efficient, and more fair, along the way, I'll be even more delighted.

SOURCES:
Brody, Paul, and Pureswaran, Veena. "The New Software -Defined Supply Chain." IBM, 2013.
    https://www.ibm.com/downloads/cas/JQP1DK0L.
Panic Blog. "The Lightning Digital AV Adapter Surprise," March 1, 2013.
    https://panic.com/blog/the-lightning-digital-av-adapter-surprise/.

CHAPTER 3

How Ethereum Works (In plain English)

I wrote this book for a non-technical audience and so I am going to deliberately avoid a deep dive into the technology that supports Ethereum. In truth, even if I wanted to write a deeply technical guide to Ethereum, I couldn't do so. My degree in Economics and my certificate in African Studies, and a lifetime in business consulting, means I just don't understand the details well enough to explain them back to you.

What I do understand are the foundational principles of software systems and, in particular, blockchains, and how those technologies can be put to use for enterprise processes. Fear not, I've had actual technical experts read over my explanations in this book and, once they have recovered from the shock of seeing things explained in simple and un-nuanced terms, they've agreed I'm describing things correctly. Or they have helped me fix my mistakes.

Here, then, I present the plain English version of how Ethereum works.

There are three foundational concepts that are useful to understand – the distributed ledger, the programmable ledger, and consensus algorithm. These three key concepts should be read alongside the next chapter, which explains the three foundational components making up the Ethereum blockchain – wallets, tokens, and smart contracts.

The Distributed Ledger

Every financial system has a ledger. The difference between Ethereum and centralized systems is that Ethereum's ledger is public and distributed to all participants. That means that thousands of copies of the Ethereum ledger exist and are being constantly updated. Every few seconds, the database that represents all these transactions receives a new batch of transactions.

Each new batch of transactions is matched with the end-point of the prior batch and a short mathematical validation takes place to ensure the new batch of transactions is part of a continuous stream of connected data. Transactions are grouped in batches for the sake of efficiency, as individually lining up millions of transactions at the same time would be too complex. Since everyone gets a copy, you may often hear blockchains referred to as "distributed ledgers."

In the world of blockchains, batches of transactions are known as blocks, and the resulting database is known as a blockchain. In many ways, there's not much about this process that is new. Batch transaction-processing is one of the oldest standardized methods used by companies to handle everything from airline reservations to bank payments. My mother spent the early part of her career as a mainframe software developer. When I explained Ethereum to her, she smartly replied that "it sounds like you people have made no progress in the last fifty years." She's not entirely wrong.

One specific practical consequence of all these database copies is that tampering with your transaction data becomes basically impossible. Sure, you can mess with your own data, but since that data is copied thousands of times, it's easy to find other sets for comparison. Consequently, you will often hear people talk about blockchains as being "tamper-proof."

Not all blockchains share this special tamper-proof quality. It is a specific practical property of public blockchains with many users and nodes. A private blockchain that has just a few users, and all the nodes run in the same company's cloud infrastructure, is easy to erase or meddle with.

The Programmable Ledger

One area with Ethereum differs from other types of ledgers is that it holds not only transactional data, but small programs as well. These programs, known as smart contracts, reside in the ledger and can be executed as needed. Because the smart contract itself resides within the ledger and can be used to define digital tokens or processes, people do sometimes refer to blockchains as "programmable ledgers" as well. Though they're not the same, the best comparable analogy for smart contracts in traditional systems is software scripts, which can be executed individually.

The Consensus Algorithm

Because blockchains do not have a centralized system for controlling the flow of transactions, the participants in the network must reach consensus on what is the valid set of transactions. The algorithm that handles this process is known as the consensus algorithm. Though there are quite a few variations across blockchains, generally this involves participants who propose new blocks of transactions while checking the math of each other participant.

In a real-world example, imagine a group of people who transact only with each other. At the start of the day, everyone has $10 each. If I give one other person $5 and I tell everyone I am giving Jane $5, then everyone knows that I now only have $5 left in my pocket and Jane now has $15. If I then announce I am giving Bob $10, everyone can immediately know that I am lying because I don't have $10 to give. If we were all to vote on whether or not this transaction should be accepted, every honest person would vote against confirming such a transaction and adding it to the ledger we each have. The consensus algorithm just takes this concept and scales it up.

Wasteful and Public

I've given this explanation roughly a million times over the last decade and, with near absolute reliability, people who are paying attention come to roughly the same two conclusions and questions each time, in roughly the same order:

The first, often, is "wow, this system only works because you have no privacy."

That's correct. Now, if you are one of millions of people and you're identified as a number not a name and you do only a few transactions, you have something sort of like anonymity and privacy in this ecosystem. For many consumers, this is "good enough" and for a few idealists, this isn't just good enough, it's perfect: transparency as a kind of social and financial disinfectant.

For business users, this immediately looks like a problem. Enterprises, by default, like to keep the details for their business operations private. Fortunately, there are work-arounds that enable privacy, and there's a whole chapter on that to come shortly. (The internet, too, started out without privacy, but it was needed to scale and make commerce work.

The second conclusion people often reach is that, "wow, this is an incredibly wasteful system."

And so it is, at least in some respects. There is nothing you can do on Ethereum that you cannot do better, faster, and cheaper, in a traditional centralized computing environment. What has changed and makes blockchains possible is that the cost of computing has fallen to nearly zero. As a result, though consensus algorithms may seem wasteful, you are spending something that is nearly free, computing power, to get something that is highly valuable: trustworthy decentralized transactions. While Ethereum came up with some very clever concepts, like smart contracts and tokenization, they're all possible in a centralized system. The sole, truly compelling value proposition for blockchain technology is decentralization, and decentralization is immensely valuable in the digital world.

This leads to the key question: why is decentralization useful and valuable?

In the pre-digital world, decentralization was largely automatic. It was not really possible for one company to span the globe. For my parents and grandparents, the pre-digital world was one with nearly endless variety. If you traveled from one country to another, everything seemed to change. Not just food and culture but even consumer products. Cars, radios, appliances, pens – there were thousands of brands that all had their unique quirks. Even multinationals like Ford weren't global companies. Ford made different cars in Europe than in the United States, even if they sometimes had the same names. The British-made Ford Escorts of my childhood I saw on summer holidays with my English grandparents were vastly different to the ones I saw at home in America.

In the pre-digital era, truly centralized national or global systems were few and far between. National banks, railroad networks, postal services, and telephone and telegraph operators were the first really big centralized systems that could act as choke points on how other businesses operated.. These were the network business models of the pre-digital era and, no surprise, they were considered so systematically important to the prosperity of a country and so strategically powerful that they were either state-owned or tightly regulated national monopolies. In nearly every major European country, governments took control of the national post office, telephone and telegraph operators, and road and rail systems. Additionally, most postal operators in Europe ran the biggest savings banks, also state controlled. Though the United States did not end up with nationally-owned phone, telegraph, and rail systems, all of these were very heavily regulated.

In the digital era, systemic global monopolies are much easier to build. No presence in most countries is required and the internet goes everywhere. Digital integration pays enormous dividends and the ability to coordinate complex business interactions is immensely valuable. Consequently, it has never been easier to build network-based businesses that scale up massively, globally, and very quickly. Just look at the pace at which ecommerce, ride-sharing, search, and social media companies have not only grown, but have also consolidated in monopolies or near-monopolies at a global level.

This process has happened with lightning speed in consumer-focused businesses. Consumers aren't typically very strategic about their planning so financial incentives and great user experience have a big impact. Very few consumers resist signing up for a system with the fear that it might mis-use their data or become a chokepoint. Enterprises, however, are strategic and it's no accident that there don't seem to be many industrial equivalents to car sharing and ecommerce. Most long-term business arrangements still flow through point-to-point systems in relatively decentralized ways.

The attraction of Ethereum to business users is that it offers all the convenience of an integrated digital business, all the value creation of a true network business model, but without a centralized market operator that can go from being a helpful integrator one day to predatory monopolist the next.

Just Like the Internet

We can already see the value of decentralization from the example of something that's so good, so cheap, and so ubiquitous almost nobody even notices it anymore: the internet. Just like Ethereum, the internet is a decentralized and permissionless network. Anyone can use it and nobody can control it. It has in a relatively short amount of time become a universal global monopoly. But, thanks to the fact that there is no central authority that controls the internet, the cost of using the internet keeps going down and the performance keeps improving.

Try to imagine what it would be like if just one company controlled the internet. We used to have something like that in our national telephone monopolies. In the 1970s and 1980s, a five-minute long-distance phone call cost as much as dinner at a nice restaurant. Phone companies used to tell customers that calling was cheaper than flying and that made it worthwhile. They were right, but it was still staggeringly expensive and, because it was a monopoly, didn't seem to get much cheaper as technology improved.

Now imagine if a single company controlled the internet. They'd tell you that $0.25 for a single email was cheaper than a stamp and much faster, so it was worth it. They would have a point, but it would still be astoundingly expensive to use. Indeed, in the 1970s and 1980s, companies that ran B2B data communications networks charged customers by the character.

Having a free, open, permissionless and decentralized internet transformed the world. The internet made phone calls and email so cheap they are, for all intents and purposes, free. It has transformed nearly every part of business life that depends on data communications. Ethereum is going to do the same for B2B commerce and everything that depends on the structured transfer of value.

So is Ethereum wasteful? I would argue "no." We're spending something that's cheap and increasingly abundant: computing power and bandwidth, to get something that's strategic and rare: open commerce without choke point operators.

CHAPTER 4

Wallets, Tokens & Smart Contracts

Wallets, tokens, and smart contracts are the main elements most enterprise users are going to interact with on the Ethereum blockchain. Understanding these three concepts and how they work together is foundational for developing a picture of how just about every business process can be modeled and managed on the blockchain.

Nearly every business agreement is a variation of an exchange of value. I've got money. You've got stuff. We're going to exchange my money for your stuff. In financial services, the exchange is a direct swap, but in most enterprise transactions, the exchange is governed by an enterprise procurement agreement. In Ethereum, both the money and the stuff can be represented as tokens while the terms of the exchange between two parties can be captured in a smart contract.

Wallets

Everything of value in the world of Ethereum is stored in a wallet. Wallets are just a name for a digital account where you can store your keys and the access rights to contracts and assets you control through those keys. What makes wallets special and important is that in a decentralized world, there's no administrator to rescue you if you lose the keys to the wallet; there is no all-powerful entity that can reverse fraudulent transactions. It's life without a safety net. Though done correctly, the risks are manageable.

All wallets have private keys and they are the most valuable items in the world of Ethereum. If you have someone's private keys, you can drain their wallet, seize their identity, and manage their contracts. It's no exaggeration to say that billions of dollars in value have been lost to poorly managed keys. For both individuals and enterprises, there are few security priorities higher than managing their wallets.

Over the last decade, a variety of approaches have emerged to managing wallets and the risks associated with a decentralized system with irrevocable transactions. Here are a few of the most important wallet concepts:

- **Hardware Wallets**: These are hardware devices that use hardware encryption and physical security to store private keys. The beauty of a hardware wallet is you can disconnect it from the blockchain and stick it in a physical vault, making theft impossible. This also makes a "cold wallet" or a "cold storage" device because transactions cannot be executed without physical connectivity to the internet.

- **Software Wallets**: More convenient and far cheaper than hardware wallets, the vast majority of end-users rely upon software wallets. These are also the most vulnerable to hacking and lost keys. Anything that's online can be hacked and manipulated.

- **Hot Wallets**: Typically the same as a software wallet – an always-on, connected wallet that can engage in a lot of transactions instantly. Convenient, but risky.

- **Cold Wallets** (AKA Cold Storage or "Air Gapped"): These are wallets that are disconnected from the internet and so cannot make transactions. Typically a hardware wallet.

- **Smart Contract Wallets**: These wallets use smart contracts that can require multiple signatures to execute transactions and can impose limits of transfers and payments at certain thresholds. Smart contract wallets address some of the big risks in self-hosted software wallets, enabling social recovery with trusted contacts and making it difficult for unauthorized users to drain an account.

- **Self-Hosted Wallets**: This is a standard type of wallet that most consumers use on the blockchain. They can be hardware or software, but either way, the end user retains total control of the wallet.

- **Hosted Wallets**: A wallet run by a third-party, such as an exchange that assumes responsibility for managing keys and many of the related risks.

- **Institutional Custody Systems**: These are enterprise-grade secure systems that mix hardware and software, hot and cold wallets and use complex cryptographic systems to manage keys across many wallets for large companies and exchanges. These are costly to implement and manage but they are essential infrastructure for firms that engage in blockchain transactions at scale. Big exchanges and digital asset holders that use institutional custody systems typically keep more than 90% of their assets in disconnected cold-wallet systems to minimize risks.

Tokens

Tokens are the native units of exchange in Ethereum – this is how value is moved around. In Bitcoin, the only tokens that existed were Bitcoins. In Ethereum, Ether is the native token, but one of the big reasons why Ethereum took off is that it allows users to define any other asset they want as a digital token as well. This has led to hundreds of thousands of tokens being created.

Tokens themselves typically come in two basic flavors: fungible and non-fungible. Fungible tokens are undifferentiated, very much like money or oil or other commodities. A dollar is a dollar, and it doesn't particularly matter which dollar you have. Non-fungible tokens are just that – they are unique and differentiated. Anything that comes in a batch, with serial numbers, or is unique, is going to be best represented as a non-fungible token.

The most common type of fungible token is the ERC-20. ERC is "Ethereum Request for Comment" – it's the Ethereum process for establishing, discussing, and setting new standards. The most common type of non-fungible token is the ERC-721. There are a staggering number of other proposed, and widely adopted standards, out there that offer some combination of fungible and non-fungible token properties and other design elements. But, for the purposes of this book, fungible and non-fungible cover all use cases without getting too far into the weeds.

Smart contracts are just pieces of code that are executed on-chain. They serve two purposes. The most common of them is to define tokens. An ERC-20 or ERC-721 contract defines the token or series of tokens.

For example, let's say you want to create a series of non-fungible tokens representing a manufactured product with a limited production run of 100,000 units. In the NFT contract, you would define a number of key characteristics including:

- Total number of NFTs that can be minted by this contract – in this case, 100,000.
- Who has authority to mint those tokens. In this case, you would probably say only the manufacturer. You could also have a scenario where you delegate minting authority to sub-contractors that you have authorized to make the product.
- Rules, if there are any, around the transfer of these tokens. For example, you may want to restrict the transfer of these tokens to authorized dealers.

- Rules for burning tokens. Burning a token means sending it to a "dead wallet" where no keys exist, making them permanently non-transferable in the future.

When people talk about blockchains as a kind of "internet of money," they are really referring to tokens that "packetize" assets, making them easily transferable. If you can tokenize an asset, you make it transactable. That means you can buy, sell, borrow and manage the asset.

One of the most useful features of blockchains for enterprise users is that they treat any token the same way banks treat money: as an item of value for which end-to-end reconciliation between parties is required and clear controls are needed. In the case of banks, you cannot just make money "appear" in your bank account. It must come from somewhere. With blockchains, the same can be true for any asset.

Take something simple like enterprise inventories. If you have manufactured products that are unique, valuable and serialized, and you represent them as digital non-fungible tokens, you can manage them on the blockchain the same as the real world.

For example, when you ship a product from the manufacturing location to a distributor, you are transferring digital tokens from your wallet to the distributor's wallet. Because the blockchain requires reconciliation, the total number of assets will have to remain the same in the transfer.

You can also treat them like financial assets. If each product has a value of $1,000 and you have 1,000 in your inventory, you have $1 million in assets represented as digital products. If your token is defined correctly, you should be able to borrow against the value of those assets to finance working capital, for example.

One critical mistake that many enterprises make in defining their tokens is failing to take a truly "blockchain-native" approach to defining these assets. Many business processes like sourcing loans or international trade tend to focus on the transfer and verification of documents. Many early blockchain projects by enterprises tried to digitize or tokenize process documents, such as bills-of-lading or loan origination documents.

The problem with this is that it's not the documents that have value; it's the assets they represent. The better approach is to tokenize the underlying asset such as the house, loan, or product and then attach documents to the tokens. (See the chapter on oracles and external information for discussion of documents and token metadata.) Now you have a natively-transactable blockchain asset.

Smart Contracts

In the most basic form, smart contracts define tokens, as covered earlier. Beyond token definition, you can use smart contracts to manage and run just about any kind of business logic, provided you can define the process with inputs, outputs and associated logic.

On Ethereum, smart contracts really got going with the launch of decentralized finance (DeFi). A single smart contract, or a network of smart contracts, could be taken and used to deliver a financial service such as taking a deposit and then paying interest on that deposit or defining a stablecoin (a digital instrument pegged to the value of an asset such as the US$) and holding collateral assets equal to the value of the coins in circulation.

One of the first really sophisticated smart contract systems put into place was the MakerDAO system for the DAI stablecoin, which made its debut in December 2017. The Dai stablecoin is what is known as an algorithmic stablecoin. The Dai is intended to be pegged in value to the U.S. dollar, but is not made up of U.S. dollars. Instead, the smart contract that governs Dai takes in other digital assets, such as ETH, the native currency of Ethereum, and then issues tokens valued at US$1.

The MakerDAO algorithm monitors the value of the U.S. dollar and the price of collateral assets in U.S. dollars and then adjusts the amount of collateral held to support those assets. Typically, you need $150 in ETH to borrow $100 in Dai. Should the value of your collateral fall below $100, the MakerDAO can "call" your loan and start liquidating the collateral.

Set aside, for the moment, the question of why this is useful, or who would want to make use of this facility, and just appreciate how complex the MakerDAO approach is to building a digital asset. This system has to handle significant volatility in the market for digital assets; it depends upon external data feeds on market prices; and automatically produces a stable asset. Since its launch at the end of December 2017, the Dai has only twice become, very briefly, unpegged from the US$1 value, a remarkable achievement in a highly volatile market.

Over the last few years, just about every major function you might expect to see in a major bank has been re-built and re-packaged as a smart contract. From deposits to lending, to index funds, they can all be handled as smart contracts. Finance has gotten here first, largely because cryptocurrencies are already fully dematerialized assets, but the principles are the same for Real World Assets (RWAs) and they can also be applied for just about enterprise business agreement.

In my own view, Smart Contracts are **the** reason for enterprises to make use of Ethereum because they allow companies to create common business processes that cross enterprise boundaries. The main way in which most companies interact with each other is by buying and selling products and services. Enterprise procurement agreements are the heart of these types of interactions and they can, for the most part, be packaged into smart contracts. Volume discounts, prices lists, and rebate rules aren't any more complex than the rules that govern many financial assets.

The Limitations & Challenges in Smart Contracts

There are, however, some important limitations and challenges associated with smart contracts that users must be aware of and manage around. The most important are security and reliability. Smart contracts are software and bug-free software isn't a realistic aspiration. There are methods to create and get to software that is nearly or completely bug free, but there are exceptionally long and costly approaches that are not practical. There is a methodology known as Formal Verification, but it isn't widely applied or easy to use at this time.

The problem with software bugs in a blockchain ecosystem is that they aren't just bothersome; they're potentially catastrophic when the smart contract is handling your money. Smart contract exploits are already responsible for billions of dollars in thefts and, though the biggest risks are manageable with proper security procedures, there is no way to reduce those risks to zero.

A second challenge is whether or not "code is law." If you have ever negotiated a contract, you know that a very small portion of the contract deals with the specific business logic on which two firms are agreeing. It only takes a page to specify things like delivery terms and volume discounts. What accounts for the endless other pages? Much of the rest of the contract involves lengthy procedures and plans for handling disagreements and the penalties for non-performance.

Neither the procedures for handling disagreements, nor penalties for non-performance, fit into an all-digital framework. Most disagreements depend on very subjective standards, such as whether or not a supplier has made a "best effort" or "reasonable effort." Similarly, the penalties for non-performance are often draconian, but rarely invoked.

Even if it was possible to fully encode all the business logic in an agreement, including dispute resolution mechanisms and penalties, doing so would probably not be a good choice. The more complex logic that is included, the more software code is required, and the more code that's required, the more opportunities there are for bugs and exploits to be implemented. Indeed, dispute resolution code would probably be in the highest risk category, since it is rarely used and so would not be easy to accumulate a huge amount of experience and testing data-points from the real world.

Two other challenges get a deeper-dive later in this book: privacy and linkages to off-chain data sources. For enterprises, the vast majority of what they do is both confidential and linked to assets or services that exist off-chain. Keeping that data private and keeping it current are both critical to making Ethereum useful and relevant.

What then, you might be wondering, is the value proposition for smart contracts in the enterprise context? The answer is they are still immensely useful, but the value proposition comes from automating routine cases, not trying to perfectly handle all the corner cases. Well-executed smart contracts contain mechanisms for the parties to agree upon changes and overrides, provided everyone agrees, and this sets the stage for off-chain dispute resolutions.

Eventually, we may get to more arms-length enterprise contracts that are entirely on-chain, but that is likely to be an evolution that takes place over time, not the "day 1" destination.

Off And Running

While there is a lot more to the Ethereum ecosystem, much of the time, business priorities will revolve around handling wallets, tokens, and smart contracts. Get those right and you are already off to a great start.

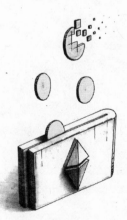

CHAPTER 5

Oracles & External Information

One of the keys to operating in a truly trustless environment is removing the necessity to depend on any external data. In the case of most traditional cryptocurrency transactions, everything you need to know about the transaction is already documented in the blockchain. The only thing you need to trust is that the math required to validate the transaction has been completed properly.

As the use-cases for blockchains expand, however, the need for external data sources becomes important. The future of blockchain technology is one where the blockchain acts as a means for managing and reconciling information about events and systems that exist off-chain. For that, external data is required. It can be as simple as the data required to complete payment on a purchase where the parties have agreed to payment upon delivery. For that, you need proof of delivery.

Oracles are inspired by Pythia of Delphi, who was a priestess who could see the future. The ancient Greeks believed that questions posed to the "Oracle of Delphi" were answered by the gods. Blockchain oracles work in a similar manner: the data that exists outside the world of Ethereum must be brought into Ethereum before it can be acted upon. Unlike Pythia, Ethereum oracles can also be used to send information to the outside world as well.

Common Applications

The most common application for oracles today are asset prices, typically crypto-asset prices. These are used to set triggers and manage trades and prices in an enormous range of applications, particularly in DeFi. A quick look at the list of Chainlink and Witnet oracles shows that over 95% are focused on asset prices. This shouldn't be surprising based on the dominance of DeFi in the blockchain ecosystem, but it's not the only purpose.

Enterprise transactions will require extensive use of oracles. From insurance policies to procurement agreements, external data will be essential to complete many smart contracts. The most common applications that are envisioned include weather data for insurance policies, logistics data for procurement and supply chain operations. While most of these are objective yes/no queries, there is no reason why oracles cannot submit more complex information. Insurance assessments are a good example: they require both a yes/no on the damage and an estimated repair cost.

Case Example: Automated Liquidations using Chainlink and AAVE

AAVE is a decentralized lending platform that allows users to earn interest on deposits and also to borrow against the value of those deposits. AAVE only allows for collateralized lending, so all borrowing must be secured with assets that can be liquidated if necessary.

AAVE requires a minimum ratio of assets to borrowing. Typically, DeFi services like AAVE require that people deposit collateral equal to 150% of the borrowed amount.

Let's use a simplified example here: Since prices for digital assets are highly volatile, it's important to have up to date pricing information that can be used to trigger liquidations if necessary. For example, if you have deposited 10 BTC when Bitcoin was worth $50,000, that means you have $500,000 in assets under deposit, enabling borrowing up to $333,333.

Imagine you borrow $250,000 in USDC (a U.S. dollar-denominated sta-blecoin). If Bitcoin falls below $37,500 based on data from Chainlink Price Feeds, AAVE will be able to automatically liquidate some of your deposits to draw down the loan amount until you are back inside the coverage range of 150% of your deposited assets.

Reality is more complex than the simplified example. Collateralized lending services have become ever more sophisticated. Their algorithms are designed to take into account market volatility and the volatility of specific assets and to reduce the risk that short, sudden price swings will have bad consequences such as triggering an unnecessary liquidation. The underlying principles remain the same.

Case Example: NBA Dynamic NFTs

A more fun case example is the NBA's use of Chainlink Oracles for their dynamic NFT collection called The Association NFT.

In this case, the NBA wanted to be able to update the content of their NFTs dynamically, adding things like trophies to the NFTs on the teams that won the 2022 NBA championship. NBA statistics are delivered on-chain using the Chainlink network and that, in turn, triggers changes to the NFT imagery and metadata. Additionally, players are assigned randomly and transparently to the NFTs using the Chainlink Verifiable Random Function.

Building & Using Reliable Oracles

Because oracles are used to trigger very important decisions on-chain, such as automating payments or liquidating loan collateral, it's critical they operate in a predictable and reliable manner. It's also important that it not be easy to fake or corrupt an oracle. If payment is triggered with proof of delivery – that proof has to be reliable.

The Ethereum Foundation says that good oracles must meet three requirements:

1. *Correctness*: An oracle should not cause smart contracts to trigger state changes based on invalid off-chain data. For this reason, an oracle must guarantee authenticity and integrity of data-authenticity means the data was gotten from the correct source, while integrity means the data remained intact (i.e., it wasn't altered) before being sent on-chain.

2. *Availability*: An oracle should not delay or prevent smart contracts from executing actions and triggering state changes. This quality requires that data from an oracle be available on request without interruption.

3. *Incentive compatibility*: An oracle should incentivize off-chain data providers to submit correct information to smart contracts. Incentive compatibility involves attributability and accountability. Attributability allows for correlating a piece of external information to its provider, while accountability bonds data providers to the information they give, such that they can be rewarded or penalized based on the quality of information provided.

Oracles are available in two main "flavors" – centralized and decentralized. Decentralized oracles often do a better job of meeting the three key criteria advanced by the Ethereum Foundation. There are multiple providers and the oracle output represents a consensus between them. Users in these decentralized oracles often have to put a "good behavior" bond (a.k.a. a "stake") in the network that can be lost for fraudulent or negligent behavior.

The problem is that for a great deal of enterprise data, there is, in fact, only one reliable source: the enterprise itself. This means there are not multiple providers who can dispute information put forward by an Oracle. In these cases, it is a good idea for enterprises to set up external audits of their reporting processes and publish those so that even where there is only a single source of the data, the process for reporting that data is independently verified.

Implementation Considerations

1. External data sources required / actions triggered
    a. What are these external data source?
    b. What kind of actions are likely to be triggered in a smart contract?
    c. What is the value of those actions?
2. Centralized or decentralized approach
    a. Are there multiple sources of the same data available?
    b. Can this application be decentralized to improve reliability?
    c. Is there only a single source for this information?
3. External verification options
    a. For single source verifications, is it common in the industry to have external audits, verifications or Systems of Control reports implemented?
    b. What kinds of external inspection could be obtained?
4. Incentive alignment
    a. What incentives exist for someone to lie or misrepresent data?
    b. How often has data been incorrect due to systems or other problems in the past?
    c. What kind of damage can be done by incorrect data?
    d. What kind of performance guarantees are appropriate?
    e. How would damage from incorrect data be fixed or compensated?

DATA SOURCES

Chainlink Blog. "77+ Smart Contract Use Cases Enabled By Chainlink," May 2019. https://blog.chain.link/smart-contract-use-cases/.

Antolin, Mike. "NBA Top Shot 101: The NFT Marketplace Allows You to Buy and Sell Original NBA Digital Content." *Coindesk*, August 23, 2022. https://www.coindesk.com/learn/nba-top-shot-101/.

Jansen, Eric. "How Oracles Make Smart Contracts Work." Finivi.com. Accessed March 5, 2023. https://www.finivi.com/oracles-make-smart-contracts-work/.

"Nexus Mutual Overview." Nexus Mutual. Accessed March 5, 2023. https://nexusmutual.io/#Overview.

O'Keefe, Adreinne. "The NBA Uses Chainlink Oracle Network and VRF To Power The Association NFT Collection." Accessed March 5, 2023. https://chain.link/case-studies/nba.

"Oracles." Ethereum Foundation, February 2022. https://ethereum.org/en/developers/docs/oracles/.

"Trigger Smart Contract Execution With Chainlink Automation." Chainlink, March 2022. https://blog.chain.link/trigger-smart-contract-execution/.

CHAPTER 6

Privacy

There is no challenge standing in the way of blockchain's potential in the enterprise more important than that of privacy. Almost every single proposed application for enterprise blockchain applications depends upon the ability for parties in the network to maintain a high degree of privacy.

Nearly every way in which most companies transact with their external business partners requires a significant level of secrecy. Just take procurement or inventory as examples – no company wants its competition to know how much it is selling, to whom, or at what price. Those are often closely guarded secrets and for public traded companies, they are material information that can affect stock prices.

Though enterprises require privacy, blockchains do not, by default, offer privacy. Though they might be based on cryptographic tools, in fact, blockchains depend upon critical data being made public to avoid having a central authority manage the system. All parties in the network are, in effect, always checking up on each other.

Nor are the traditional tools that are used to provide some limited elements of privacy for consumers particularly useful for most enterprise applications. There are many different privacy solutions available, nearly all of them designed for individuals using fungible assets and they are not suitable for enterprise users. Using pseudo-anonymous addresses instead of names, or trading through an exchange, allows consumers to hide their identity and transactions to a degree. Your transaction of a completely fungible token is one of many in a large stream of data.

Enterprise users often do three things that will end up giving away a great deal of information about what they are doing and rendering most consumer-focused privacy solutions useless:

- **Large volumes of transactions**. A typical high volume industrial client that I have worked with produces about 500,000 units of a particular

SKU each day. These kinds of volumes will quickly make you highly visible in a large blockchain environment.

- **Non-fungible assets**. Most industrial products and services are non-fungible. Even millions of identical phones or cars end up being represented as non-fungible tokens because they have serial numbers or batch identifiers. A mobile phone from one company is not the same as a mobile from another. NFTs are easy to track across the blockchain in public.

- **Business Logic**. Large companies typically establish long-term agreements with each other that involve business rules such as volume discounts, standardizing pricing, or rebates at certain purchasing volumes. The logic in those contracts is, itself, highly sensitive and, in their default configurations, readable by any party on the network.

As a result of these restrictions, only a very tiny subset of enterprise blockchain applications can be implemented without privacy. These are often simplified applications like product traceability where whole batches of product get assigned a single identifier.

Enter Zero-Knowledge Proofs

This book isn't a math class and I'm not qualified to teach one, but encryption and privacy technology depends on some very advanced math. The most important kind, for the purposes of this discussion, are zero-knowledge proofs. The fundamental concept is that you can prove an assertion to be true without revealing the underlying data behind that assertion.

I've heard quite a few good explanations of how these work, in plain English, but the best I have seen so far is this. Imagine you are color-blind but your friend asserts that the two balls in your hand are, in fact, different colors. To you, they look identical. He says he can prove this is true by having you hold one ball in each hand, hide your hands behind your back and either switch them or not switch them. When you put your hands back in front of you, your friend will be able to tell if you have swapped them or not. If your friend can tell you three times in a row the correct answer, he has proven beyond a reasonable doubt that they are in fact different.

The clever thing about this little example is when you're done, you still don't know which ball is red or blue, or what red or blue even looks like. Truly you have zero-knowledge of the answer, but you can and do believe that they are different colors.

Nightfall

Practically speaking, there are two privacy mechanisms that we need to create to support enterprise applications. The first is a "dark pool" where we can exchange assets and payments under privacy. This is known as a Shield Contract because information inside the contract is shielded. You can put assets into these contracts and take them out. That part is publicly visible to everyone on the blockchain. For assets that exist inside this shield contract, however, it is not possible to determine with whom you are transacting or what you are doing with them.

In addition to moving assets in and out of Shield Contracts, it is also possible to create assets inside a shield contract and then "export" them into the world of blockchain. (This works for assets that have a value in the real world and can be associated with real-world assets. But is not entirely kosher with the spirit of blockchain if you want to use it for a true digital-native crypto-asset, as it violates the idea that asset creation is tightly controlled in those instances.) For most enterprise users, however, they will likely want to keep all assets inside the Shield Contract at all times to preserve their privacy and most of those assets will have a "real world" linkage as well.

In the case of asset movements, the main privacy solution I am familiar with is Nightfall. Nightfall is a blockchain privacy technology that was originally created by EY and donated into the public domain. Nightfall is a shield contract that runs as a Zero-Knowledge Optimistic Roll-Up – often referred to as an ZK Optimistic Roll-Up. Now let me unpack that. We've already discussed the Zero-Knowledge component, and to that foundation we added three additional components.

First, Nightfall is a "roll-up," which means that it consolidates transactions inside the privacy environment and anchors them on the Ethereum Blockchain. This means that assets can easily move in and out of the shield contract without "leaving" the Ethereum blockchain. Transactions are summarized and connected to the main-net.

Secondly, we chose an Optimistic solution. Optimistic solutions are just that – they assume, optimistically, that other actors are good. This means that instead of requiring every transaction to be verified by everyone else, it assumes that transactions are valid. To prevent bad actors, transactions are locked for seven days to give others time to independently verify them and challenge them on-chain if they are invalid. In practice, there are solutions to allow expedited withdrawals with additional confirmation. The key benefit of this solution is that it drastically reduces that amount of Ethereum "gas" needed to process transactions as the process for challenges runs only by exception.

Finally, Nightfall requires that participants have an enterprise X.509 identity certificate to access the privacy shield. These certificates are closely related to the Secure Sockets Layer (SSL) certificates that are widely used to secure the public internet, but are focused on the identity of an organization and the signing individual as well. This means that the network users are identifiable, though the details of their transactions are not.

The decision to require an X.509 certificate was a design compromise that I supported. While I strongly believe in the value of privacy, nobody on our team or the others with whom we worked on this open source and public-domain solution wanted it to become a pathway for money laundering or other unconstructive activities. The process of obtaining an identity certificate is not difficult, but it does require that companies identify themselves and that their documentation is run through the major sanctions screenings processes.

Nightfall is designed to be a full public, permissionless and open ecosystem. The underlying code base for Nightfall has been placed entirely in the public domain, so no licenses or rules are attached to using or modifying the technology. Additionally, X.509 certificates are a public, open standard and there are many firms that offer this service, so there is no single entity that becomes a "gatekeeper" controlling access.

Starlight

The second privacy mechanism that is needed is the ability to execute business logic. If you go back to the basic model of how enterprises operate, they exchange money for products or services under the terms of an agreement. The underlying terms of the agreement are themselves sensitive. A volume discount that kicks in at 1 million units already tells you a lot about the kinds of volumes that a company is going to buy or the product volumes that they plan to put into the market.

As with private payments and transfers, zero-knowledge proofs can be leveraged to enable business rules to be implemented. All the transactions under the contract are represented as leaves in a large mathematical tree (a Merkle Tree).

Because each company has customized business relationships with other parties, it's not possible to create a generic shared privacy environment for all enterprise contracts the way it is for simple payments and transfers in Nightfall. As a result, each new contract has to be developed individually, and that's where the Starlight came from.

Developing customized zero-knowledge circuits turns out to be difficult, even for professional programmers. Our team failed in several efforts to "teach" this skill and instead decided to develop a "transpiler" that can convert

Ethereum Solidity contracts to zero-knowledge circuits and Starlight was born. With some relatively minor modifications, you can convert a solidity contract to a zero-knowledge circuit.

As with Nightfall, Starlight outputs a Shield Contract. Assets can go into and come out of this shielded zone. Whereas the logic in Nightfall is standardized for everyone, the logic in a Starlight-created Shield Contract is customized to the specific contract.

Starlight contracts are not Optimistic contracts, at least at the time of writing, which means they do incur much larger gas fees. They are probably best deployed on side-chains where gas fees are much lower.

As with Nightfall, Starlight is in the public domain and available for anyone to use without licenses or restrictions.

Starfall & The Complications of Privacy

There is no such thing as perfect privacy. The goals of Nightfall and Starlight are to allow enterprise users to keep their sensitive business information from the competition, not regulators. That doesn't mean that there are any back doors in the code. There aren't. The code is also fully open-source and in the public domain, which means anyone can read and modify the code as needed as well.

But there is no design for privacy that doesn't leak some data. This is no different than in the real world. When Apple launches a new phone, it's quite common for competitors and journalists to buy one, rip it open, and start identifying the suppliers and estimating costs. Satellite images are used to count trucks at depots, cars in parking lots, and ships in ports. There's no business that doesn't "leak" data.

In using privacy systems like Nightfall and Starlight, we've had to accept some limitations, but there are still ways to maximize privacy. On the limitations side, there is really no way to hide your usage of these systems. Identification requirements mean that if you use Nightfall, regulators can see that, and while your competition cannot see what you are doing, it does make Nightfall unattractive for bad actors. An analogy from the industrial world is that everyone knows that Apple and Google buy chips from TSMC and Samsung. That's not a secret. What is a secret is how many, what they pay for them, and when they're to be delivered and for what product.

In the case of Nightfall, if many companies come to use the system, it will quickly become impossible to understand who is doing business with whom. Companies that put money or assets into or take them out of Nightfall will be visible, but their actions within Nightfall will not.

The same cannot be said for Starlight. Since Starlight produces customized smart contracts, they might be used with far fewer participants. Imagine a complex business agreement between a buyer and seller with a lot of rules about prices and rebates. In the end, though the logic and data inside the contract are private, if you are seen putting $1 million dollars into the system and taking out 100,000 widget tokens, no matter how sophisticated the logic, I can pretty quickly guess your average price per widget.

You can, of course, create and keep all tokens inside the contract. And that might be fine in some cases, but if these widgets are batteries and they go into smartphones, now I need to extract the battery widgets from a custom Starlight contract and move them into Nightfall. At this point, I've now leaked so much data my efforts at privacy were pointless.

To deal with these complex multi-party supply chains, we need something more: Starfall, which is exactly what it sounds like. ~~The end of human civilization.~~ Starfall allows you to execute private, customized business logic inside of a customized Starlight contract but create and manage the movement of tokens in the much larger privacy pool of Nightfall.

No End in Sight

Though we have to start small with relatively simpler logic, I am confident that over time, we and other companies and people will master the challenges of privacy on public blockchains. As the capabilities mature, we will be able to build ever more complex logic and manage ever larger connected chains of business interactions, all without having to disclose sensitive information to a third party.

The future is one where all B2B interactions can be easily, simply, and privately secured on the public Ethereum network.

CHAPTER 7

Scaling Ethereum – Layer 1, 2 and Beyond

Decentralized transaction-processing is complicated. Every transaction effectively gets copied to the nearly 10,000 different public nodes on Ethereum and transactions are verified by a complex consensus process. The result is that it can take time for transactions to be verified, the precise order of transactions being verified isn't aligned with the time stamp, and the network has limited capacity.

For the purposes of most enterprise transactions, issues like transaction time, sequence, and finality are not that important. While financial firms care a great deal about rapid execution, most companies think about cycle time and operations in terms of days, not seconds, so some of the constraints that exist in blockchains like Ethereum today on time and speed are not so critical.

What does matter a great deal is scalability. Ethereum that exists today and has existed for around a decade now can handle about a million transactions a day. That's not remotely close to enough for business users. I have clients that want to do as many as two million a day for one product. Obviously, the default isn't nearly enough.

Fortunately, scalability has been an obsession with the Ethereum community since very early on and, starting in 2021, there have been viable options to handle tens of millions or even billions of transactions a day.

There are four major paths to scaling that are worth knowing about:

Sharding: Ethereum's own core roadmap includes a transition to sharding. Sharding is a database technique that allows you to split an integrated database into multiple "shards." Each shard is a piece of the database that can both operate independently and be reconciled and integrated with the others. This is a common scaling technique for large centralized systems that need to partially run in parallel. Sharding on Ethereum is forecast to be a gradual transition starting in 2023.

Side Chains: Side chains mimic the structure of the Ethereum main network, allowing people to execute smart contracts and move tokens back and forth, but do so independently. Side chains like the Polygon Proof of Stake network are often optimized for much more transaction throughput, though at the cost of less security compared to Ethereum. These are a great choice for higher volume transaction applications. Polygon's PoS network, the most popular, can handle upwards of 25 million transactions a day.

Roll-Ups: These systems summarize a large block group of transactions on the Ethereum mainnet in a single transaction. Roll-ups come in two flavors: optimistic and zero-knowledge roll-ups. Optimistic roll ups are, as the name suggests, optimistic. They assume that transactions are valid and complete them without additional verification. You typically have a week to review and challenge transactions before they are finalized and everyone using the system essentially has to put a "good behavior" bond that can be forfeit for falsifying data. The lack of additional verification makes these systems cheap and scalable, but the price is paid in the verification delay.

Zero-Knowledge roll-ups use advanced math to verify transactions and bundle them together. The math and computation are more complex, and so the transaction fees on-chain can be higher, but the payoff is faster finality for the transactions.

Layer 2 Chains: While roll-ups can only summarize transactions, layer 2 chains allow users to execute complex smart contracts and then summarize the results on Ethereum. As with roll-ups, chains come in both optimistic and zero knowledge varieties. Layer 2 chains are far more complex, however, and much less mature at the time of this writing.

Privacy Roll-Ups: While there are no privacy layer 2 fully enabled "chains" yet, there are two privacy roll-ups at the time of this writing. Aztec is a privacy enabled ZK roll-up. Nightfall, developed primarily by EY, is a ZK-Optimistic roll-up that uses zero knowledge math for privacy purposes and adds an optimistic component to keep transaction costs down.

Fast & Slow Progress

Very slow progress on Ethereum scalability has been perhaps the single biggest source of frustration among developers and users in the Ethereum ecosystem. In years past, it was a single largest objection I faced with enterprise users looking at public networks.

When Ethereum gets congested, transaction fees can skyrocket. At peak times in the past, it's not been unusual to pay $35-50 to execute a single transaction. That would have made any large scale supply chain or business operation hopelessly uneconomic.

The slow progress of Ethereum's scalability is related to the "herding cats" nature of the organization itself. Decentralized systems evolve slowly based on a broad consensus among users and developers. For the most part, I see this as a positive thing. The last thing you want to do is trust your mission-critical business operations to an ecosystem that has a "move fast and break things" philosophy. The thing that will get broken is your business.

The good news is Ethereum has been making quite consistent progress. The network typically gets upgraded about three-four times a year. Sometimes, as with the transition from Proof of Work to Proof of Stake, this happens with a lot of fanfare. Usually, these network hard forks take place without any user even noticing. The Ethereum Foundation oversees a boring, tedious, and lengthy testing program for all "hard fork" upgrades. It's the best kind of boring and tedious you can get.

The structure of Ethereum fortunately does allow for very rapid and iterative progress by third parties, however. The explosion of the layer 2 ecosystem of roll-ups and chains is proof of this. Prototype environments started arriving in 2020 and production quality systems started arriving in 2021. By October 2022, more transactions were consistently being executed on various Layer two networks than on the Ethereum foundation (Layer 1) network.

Even with sharding and other improvements in the Ethereum roadmap, my own expectation is that the future of Ethereum is as a blockchain that really connects other blockchains. These chains and roll-ups will offer a huge variety of execution environments and value propositions that will allow businesses to find the right mix of security, privacy, speed and cost for their particular applications.

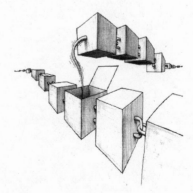

CHAPTER 8

Why Ethereum

When I was a young IBM executive, my boss once explained IBM's leadership philosophy as dictatorship tempered by assassination. I think I got the message: I needed to either get with his program or have him assassinated. There are not a lot of assassinations in the IBM offices, but you can be re-assigned overseas. It's cleaner and just as effective.

This turns out to be a pretty good explanation of how technology ecosystems work as well. Over and over again, we see ecosystems where there is a single large player and then perhaps a few smaller ones clinging on with specialized applications. In the case of blockchains, we now have a clear winner, Ethereum.

Early-Stage Cambrian Explosion

To understand how we got here and where things are likely to go, it's useful to look at the history of other technology ecosystems. The evolution always starts with some early innovations that appear to create an entirely new category of product. Not long after the first computers came into existence, the need to connect them created the business of computer networking. Computers themselves went through multiple phases, from mainframes, to minicomputers, to PCs, and then to phones. Smartphones make a great case study of how early ecosystems grow explosively and then how they mature into hardened categories with dominant market leaders.

The early-stage explosion of smartphone innovation began in 1995, long before we knew to call them Smartphones. IBM built the world's first. Called "Simon" and marketed in cooperation with Bell South, it had limited functionality and cost an absurd amount of money. IBM's Simon came out in 1995 and sold just 50,000 units. Nokia followed suit in 1996 with the Nokia 9000. Blackberry launched its 850 model in 1996 as well, though it was not yet a phone, just a two-way email device.

In 2001, smartphones represented less than 5% of the global mobile phone market, but Research In Motion, the maker of Blackberry phones, was taking off. By the time the iPhone launched in 2007, the market was just over a decade old and Blackberry and Palm and Nokia lead the market. The first Android phone arrived in 2008. At that time, about a quarter of all phones sold were smartphones and the market was accelerating rapidly. The period between 2008 and 2012 was the peak of the market evolution, when a huge number of different options were available to consumers.

It was not going to last, however. Today, Android's share of the smartphone market is greater than 75% worldwide. Apple's share is about 24%. And all the other choices amount to under 1% of total smartphone sales worldwide.

A great visual illustration of the Cambrian Explosion of the PC market is illustrated here below (with permission from Asymco.com). Please keep in mind that the chart is the log scale, so even small differences on the chart amount to millions of devices. As early as 1984, the MS-DOS (soon to be Windows) PC was the dominant platform, though competition kept arriving for years and the last alternatives other than the Mac didn't exit the market for another decade.

Software Economics and Network Effects

Two key "laws" drive the technology market towards dominance by just one or two entities. The first is Metcalf's Law. Metcalf's Law says that the value of any network is equal to the square of the number of users on the network. That means, quite simply, that networks with more users become exponentially more valuable than their competition.

This was meant to apply to actual computer networks, but it turns out to work equally well for anything that has a network effect. App stores and instant messengers are both good examples. Indeed, the immense popularity of Blackberry Messenger is thought to have done much to slow Blackberry's collapse after Android and iOS became so powerful as die-hard users held on to their messaging networks of friends and family.

The second "law" is one that says that the marginal cost of software is zero. That means that if you are an incumbent in the market and have already spent the sunk cost to develop high quality software, you can add new members to your network by selling your product at a very low price, since it costs you nothing more to make one more copy.

The combination of low entry pricing and "sticky" network effects makes it exceptionally hard to dislodge incumbents in a marketplace once they get a significant lead on others in an ecosystem. The greater your value that comes from others in the market, and the larger the share of your product that is software, the faster you can achieve sustainable market dominance.

Online marketplaces, which are all about software and the network effect of buyers and sellers, are very powerful. This is a perfect description of a typical software app store environment. By contrast, cars, though increasingly dependent on software, still have a lot of hardware that has real costs and your car doesn't become more valuable simply because other cars on the road are the same make and model. The result is that software is susceptible to being dominated by single firms and products. Microsoft Windows is a good example: it has 76% of the global PC market.

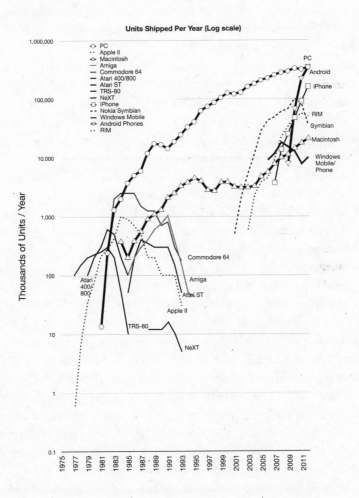

Chart by Horace Dediu, used with permission.

Blockchains tend towards the more extreme end of this spectrum. They are really valuable only as networks for transferring products and services and they are entirely composed of software. For that reason, I expect that Ethereum will indeed become the dominant blockchain ecosystem and it's also why I don't believe in the "multi-chain hypothesis" you often hear about from "industry experts." That's why I have never invested in cross-chain connectivity.

Good Enough Technology & The Ten-Year Window

At some point, markets seem to shift from an experimental phase in absorbing new technologies towards one where a single standard or market leader starts to take off and become dominant. I believe this happens when the use case starts to take precedence over the technological novelty and the buyers behavior changes.

In the world of enterprise mainframe computing, this seems to have happened when mainframes were widely adopted for handling large scale transaction processing. IBM's first big "hit" with early mainframes were utilities, insurers, banks, and airlines, all looking to efficiently handle millions of customers doing routine, repetitive transactions. Mainframe computers drastically reduced costs and increased reliability.

Spreadsheets (Visicalc, then Lotus 1-2-3, and finally Excel) drove early PC adoption and email was the "killer" application for the Blackberry. In the case of blockchain technology, decentralized finance (DeFi) and NFTs seem to have turned what was something of a technical curiosity for a small group of cryptocurrency enthusiasts into mainstream applications.

In many technology ecosystems, market leaders seem to emerge within about a decade of the product category being born. MS-DOS, soon to be MS-Windows was the leading PC operating system by 1984, about eight years after the first PCs emerged. iOS came into existence just about a decade after the smartphone category emerged. From office productivity (Microsoft), network equipment (Cisco), to cloud computing (Amazon), the pattern repeats.

One of the most challenging aspects of looking at any technology ecosystem is figuring out why the best products never seem to win. Microsoft Windows, in 1984, was terrible. Not just by today's standards, but even compared to some of the other excellent options available at the time, including the Mac. But there were many others, like the Atari ST series and the Commodore Amiga, with more modern underpinnings and better user interfaces.

My hypothesis here is that once the technology reaches a "good enough" stage, better technological foundations don't trump the "killer use case." Spreadsheets and word processing on Windows worked "well enough" and the companies that made and sold PCs, which was primarily IBM in 1984, were good at serving the main buyers, other enterprises. The combination of "good enough" technology and enterprise services was enough to tip the scales.

The same kind of experience is being repeated today in the world of blockchain. Over and over again, new Layer 1 blockchain networks are launched that claim to offer vastly better performance than Ethereum: more transactions, lower costs, and faster finality. In the end, this doesn't seem to matter compared to value that is locked in the Ethereum ecosystem with thousands of applications and developers and billions of dollars of capital.

The world of blockchain and smart contract platforms is now over a decade old. Bitcoin is t13, and the earliest versions of Ethereum date from 2014 and 2015. In the last year, Ethereum has seen off nearly all its main challenges and executed a major upgrade from Proof of Work to Proof of Stake. Short of a major screw-up by the collective leadership of the Ethereum ecosystem, it's likely to continue in the dominant market position.

One thing to note, however, is that the losers don't go quietly or quickly. Microsoft may have emerged as the market leader for office productivity suites all the way back in 1993, but IBM didn't give up on Lotus 1-2-3 until 2013. As late as 2015, when I left IBM for the second time, I was still getting the occasional 1-2-3 spreadsheet from old-timers instead of Excel. Blackberry's market share of the global mobile business actually peaked two years after the iPhone debuted and didn't fall below 5% until 2013.

For those same reasons, we can expect many of the unsuccessful "Ethereum killers" to be around for years to come. It won't change the outcome, but it will contribute to a lot of noise in the market.

Continuously Evolving Use Cases

Once a new technology finds a set of use cases that drive initial adoption, a technology ecosystem enters a period of mainstream adoption. But the evolution of that ecosystem doesn't end there. At some point, the network itself becomes the use case – the fact that "everyone" is on it and has access to the same core infrastructure becomes more important than the original use case.

Spreadsheets are still widely used, but most people have PCs for a huge variety of tasks and new applications are often launched on PCs or over the internet simply because they are widely available. Indeed, the value of a network is so great that it can overpower other challenges. Phone calls and video conferences over the internet are a great example: The internet doesn't have "quality of service" or any foundational way to prioritize one kind of information over another. That's terrible for calls, but, because everyone has a PC or phone with a network connection and a camera, it's easier and simpler to put up with spotty connections than build a new network.

And so it will be with Ethereum. The existence of a vast global network where millions of people and companies have assets and can make business transactions with each other will, over time, become more important than the particular features of the network, and so the use cases will continue to grow and evolve.

Ethereum today has accrued the most capital and has the most active developers, participants and infrastructure providers. This means that is already the easiest ecosystem in which to develop and in which to find skills and assets that speed up the solution development process and on which people can build evolving use cases.

Some Monopolies Are Better Than Others

If all network-based businesses are natural monopolies, why does it matter which one wins? The answer is that open, decentralized monopolies are not the kind of monopoly that users and enterprises need to worry about. Centralized, Web 2.0 monopolies turned out to be great at building the infrastructure of digital markets and connecting buyers and sellers. But, once they matured into stable monopoly-like market leaders, their business models tended to turn towards extracting value from the ecosystem.

Digitizing commerce is immensely valuable and in the economic model that drives stock-market valuations, growth is always required. The most profitable way to grow is to extract more value from your customer base. If you run a market that connects buyers and sellers, that means charging more, but it also means mining the data in the transaction information to develop new businesses. From consumer auctions to retail to ride-sharing, it's a familiar pattern.

The internet itself is a form of monopoly that has gotten cheaper over time. We're not used to thinking about the internet as a monopoly, but it is. In the 1990s, there were many available network choices. Today, there's only one. And while people do complain about the cost of internet access (often delivered by monopoly cable TV and telecom operators), the internet itself is only getting cheaper and better and it has no serious challengers.

The difference is that the internet is an open, permissionless, and decentralized monopoly. Anyone can join, contribute, and use it. There is no central authority in a position to control access, decide which applications can be used, or to mine or access transactional data. The result is an endlessly innovative ecosystem.

Public blockchains like Ethereum follow the same model as the internet: they are public, permissionless and decentralized systems. Because it is a network model, it is destined to be a monopoly. But, if we are going to end up putting our business models on a monopoly network, a public and permission-less monopoly is the only kind worth having.

Of course, nothing is forever. I think Ethereum, like many major technology standards, could be around for a very long time. That being said, eventually, something drastically better, newer, or just entirely different and more useful will come along. Then the market leader will be replaced. As my old boss said, dictatorship tempered by assassination.

BIBLIOGRAPHY

McCracken, Harry (April 2, 2012). "25 Years of IBM's OS/2: The Strange Days and Surprising Afterlife of a Legendary Operating System." Time Magazine. Retrieved 20 May 2017. https://techland.time.com/2012/04/02/25-years-of-ibms-os2-the-birth-death-and-afterlife-of-a-legendary-operating-system/

Darrow, Barbara. "Whatever Happened To Lotus 1-2-3?" *ChannelWeb*, January 2, 2002. https://web.archive.org/web/20090109203535/http://www.crn.com/it-channel/18818026.

Dediu, Horace. "Platform Market Share Over Time." Industry Analysis. Accessed January 23, 2023. http://www.asymco.com.

Eagle, James. "How the Mobile Phone Market Has Evolved Over 30 Years." Reference Data, May 3, 2022. https://www.visualcapitalist.com/cp/how-mobile-phone-market-has-evolved-since-1993/.

Deseret News. "LOTUS UNVEILS ITS VERSION OF POPULAR SPREADSHEET FOR IBM MAINFRAME USERS," February 27, 1990. https://www.deseret.com/1990/2/28/18849012/lotus-unveils-its-version-of-popular-spreadsheet-for-ibm-mainframe-users.

"Nokia Communicator." In *Wikipedia*. Accessed January 29, 2023. https://en.wikipedia.org/wiki/Nokia_Communicator.

Sager, Ira. "Before IPhone and Android Came Simon, the First Smartphone." *Bloomberg*, June 29, 2012. https://www.bloomberg.com/news/articles/2012-06-29/before-iphone-and-android-came-simon-the-first-smartphone#xj4y7vzkg.

Statcounter Global Stats. "Mobile Operating System Market Share North America." Accessed January 29, 2023. https://gs.statcounter.com/os-market-share/mobile/north-america.

Statista. "Market Share of Major Office Productivity Software Worldwide as of February 2022." Reference Data, January 29, 2023. https://www.statista.com/statistics/983299/worldwide-market-share-of-office-productivity-software/.

"Smartphone Sales Forecasts in the United States from 2005 to 2022." Reference Data. Accessed January 23, 2003. https://www.statista.com/statistics/191985/sales-of-smartphones-in-the-us-since-2005/.

II.

BUSINESS
USE
CASES
&
CASE
STUDIES

CHAPTER 9

General Use Case Considerations

I've tried to organize this section on use cases in a way that moves from foundational solutions towards the more complex use cases.

The early chapters in this section are focused on use cases such as notarizing documents, tokenizing assets, or making payments. To do something more advanced like procurement, for example, you need a smart contract to connect the making and movement of products, represented by digital asset tokens, in exchange for payments, often in stablecoins.

That being said, I've done my best to avoid jargon so if you care most deeply about supply chain management, you ought to be able to skip directly to the relevant chapter first and then come back to others as needed.

Each chapter has a somewhat similar structure: an overview of the value proposition, some key considerations when implementing solutions, a couple of case examples, if they are available, followed by a discussion of the limitations and challenges involved.

Most of these chapters end with short checklists of useful questions to ask as you consider implementation choices or options. These are not meant to be comprehensive, but rather as useful thought-starters in a larger process of detailed design.

CHAPTER 10

Notarization and Document Verification

Notarizing documents or information on public blockchains can bring significant value to supply chain management. By leveraging the decentralized and immutable nature of blockchain technology, companies can increase efficiency, reduce the risk of fraud, and improve overall trust in the business ecosystem. Notarization is often the first thing that companies do, presenting a simple, low-risk, and low-cost first step into the world of blockchain.

When a document is notarized on a blockchain, it is hashed and added as a transaction. Hashing a document is a process of converting the document into a fixed-size string of characters, also known as a hash. The hash is unique to the document and is generated using a mathematical function, known as a cryptographic hash function.

The hash function takes the document as input and produces a hash as output. The hash is a one-way process, meaning that it is not possible to recreate the original document from the hash. However, any changes to the document will result in a different hash, making it easy to detect whether the document has been altered.

When a document is "notarized" on a blockchain, the document itself is hashed and the hash is placed on-chain as part of a transaction, not the whole document. This is much more efficient and also preserves privacy better, so the original cannot be retrieved from the blockchain.

Value Proposition

The main benefit of notarizing documents on a blockchain is the ability to create a tamper-proof record of transactions and documents. This has a huge range of applications, which all revolve around basically similar conditions: the importance of having proof that an original document can be verified.

Some of the more sophisticated visions for applying notarizing involve having critical third parties attach documentation required to complete smart contracts. But, in practice, this is not yet done in commercial contracts. The main obstacle is that standard smart contracts themselves lack privacy and therefore few companies want to make the details of their contract agreements public.

Over the years, I have spoken to several companies that envision using notarization as part of a business contract process. The notarized documents can be used as proof that work has been completed in industries like construction, where contract payments are often based on specific project milestones. I am yet to see any of these come together and scale up, however.

The most typical operational implementation has been either in marketing, with many companies using notarization to record batch, or product history, without disclosing total volumes or other sensitive information.

Case Example: Casa Girelli Wines, Italy

The very first client for which EY built a notarization solution was Casa Girelli (Cavit Company Group) in Italy. Casa Girelli is one of the biggest wine makers in Italy and has been working for years to increase the profile of their wines globally. One of their biggest challenges has been to convey the quality of their wines, proving biological origin and the authenticity in export markets where wine counterfeiting has become common.

Its solution was to start from data gathering of the information from the production process, generating documentation around their wines and the origin. This data was then packaged up and notarized using blockchain technology to verify the authenticity of the documents and, hence, the wine.

Each Casa Girelli bottle gets a QR code on the label that takes users to their web site. From the website, which is muti-lingual, buyers can read about the wine, understand good food pairings, and see sourcing information about regions and wineries. They can also verify the authenticity of the documents by checking them against the Ethereum blockchain. (The original project was on Ethereum, but as transaction fees have risen, they have moved to the Polygon Proof of Stake side-chain.)

Since starting this project in 2017, Casa Girelli has notarized and documented data on millions of bottles of wine and has seen user engagement soar. Every customer who uses the QR code to read about the product or food pairings is deepening their relationship with the winery. It estimates that the program generates a 15% annual ROI and increases the value of the wine in the customers' eyes. Casa Girelli found that customers are willing to pay as much as a 40% price premium for verifiable products in businesses or regions where counterfeiting is high.

Overall, the program has been a big success. If there is a downside, however, it is that notarization doesn't support structured data such as volumes of specific assets, and it can provide only a simple "yes/no" answer. For companies using this in supply chain traceability, that means having a separate system for public traceability while maintaining a confidential, granular system for structured supply chain data. As a result, for most companies, notarization is a step on a process towards using public blockchains, not an end goal.

Case Example: Combatting Fake News with Document Notarization

One case where there is long-term value and significant scalability from notarization is in verification is where the yes/no answer is needed and useful at scale. So far, the most compelling example of this I have seen is with ANSA, the largest independent news gathering organization in Italy and the fifth largest in the world. Every day, every article published by Ansa is hashed and documented on the Polygon Proof of Stake Network.

Readers can follow a link at the bottom of each story, which takes them to a custom web page, from which they can check the hash and even look at the specific hashing record on the Polygon blockchain and verify the history and publishing date. Finalized articles are sent to a server maintained by EY where they are hashed, the hash is posted to the blockchain, and then the hash information is attached to the article for publication.

The system, which uses EY's OpsChain application, has been in place since 2020 and has processed over 1 million original news articles a year since going live with notarizations taking place on the Polygon Proof of Stake side-chain to keep transaction costs down at such high volumes.

In May of 2022, this solution got a real test when hackers broke the Ansa site security and used it to try to distribute misinformation. The Ansa-check banners were missing and broken in falsified articles helping users verify that there were not real.

Solution Design, Considerations, & Limitations

One of the advantages of document notarization as a solution strategy is that it works with both public and private information. The actual document contents do not need to be disclosed to anyone, only the hash, and there is no way to re-create the original document from the hash. You are then set up for easy verification and an answer to a simple yes or no question does the copy match the original.

There are a few downsides to this approach. The lack of complexity enabled is one issue – only the yes or no question can be answered. Additionally, even the yes or no question can be hard to correctly implement as the document in question needs to be an exact copy. This works nicely with digital documents, which can be copied and reproduced exactly, but not with analog documents that never scan or copy precisely the same way. For digital documents, even the smallest change in the contents will result in a complete mismatch.

While no blockchain enables you to attach the full document efficiently, one option that is also available is to attach a URL to the blockchain transaction, allowing users to retrieve the document and check the hash directly. The document itself can either be public or private and stored in a public or private cloud infrastructure. Decentralized, tamper-proof storage systems like ARWeave and the Interplanetary File System (IPFS) are starting to gain wide usage in this way.

Future Path

The future path of document notarization is integration into smart contracts with the help of third parties. Once smart contracts are privacy-enabled, inspection services and delivery services will be able to provide documents and verification into the contracting process, triggering the release of funds or other steps in the business process. For many applications, however, the future direction is a shift to privacy-enabled tokenization that supports much more granular business operations.

Implementation Considerations

1. Intended results, audience, and return on investment.
    a. Audience
    b. ROI
2. Document definition
    a. What is the document to be notarized?
    b. What is the document format being used? Is it digital or analog?
        i.   Only digital documents are well suited for hashing and notarization.
    c. What is the Yes/No question that will be answered by comparing the original document to the copy and the document hash?
        i.   How will the verifier receive an exact copy of the document? Does the verifier need to have instructions on how to package or compile the document to create an exact match?
3. Source data systems and integration plans
    a. What is the source data being used for the documents?
    b. Are the documents being produced in a consistent manner that

        makes verification reliable?

   c. What, if any, external verifications are needed to make this solution credible? What tests will you perform to make sure it is working well? Will you hire an external firm or an audit firm to verify these results and possibly public a SOC report?

4. Privacy and security requirements

   a. Will the documents that are being hashed be generally publicly available or are the documents private?

   b. How will you distribute the documents if they are public or private?

5. End user access

   a. How will end users access and easily verify the correct information? Will there be a user-friendly landing page from a QR code, a link to a blockchain explorer, or a transaction number?

   b. If off-chain data is required, how will this be handled? Will it be on an immutable off-chain data system such as IPFS or on a more traditional access-controlled cloud infrastructure?

BIBLIOGRAPHY

"ANSA Leveraging Blockchain Technology to Help Readers Check Source of News," June 4, 2020. https://www.ansa.it/english/news/science_tecnology/2020/04/06/ansa-using-blockchain-to-help-readers_af820b4f-0947-439b-843e-52e114f53318.html.

Ledger Insights. "EY Helps Italy's ANSA News Agency Use Blockchain to Fight Covid-19 Fake News," April 20, 2020. https://www.ledgerinsights.com/ey-ansa-news-agency-blockchain-covid-19-fake-news/.

University of Arkansas, Sam Walton School of Business, Blockchain Center of Excellence. "Fake News Catches the Eye – ANSAcheck Is Now a Teaching Case Study," July 29, 2021. https://blockchain.uark.edu/fake-news-catches-the-eye-ansacheck-is-now-a-teaching-case-study/.

EY Global Blockchain. "How Blockchain Helps the Public See the Truth in the Story." Accessed August 2, 2023. https://www.ey.com/en_gl/consulting/how-blockchain-helps-the-public-see-the-truth-in-the-story.

Perrone, Giuseppe. "Restoring Trust in the Wine Industry, from Grape to Glass." *EY Global Blockchain* (blog). Accessed August 2, 2023. https://www.ey.com/en_lu/global-review/2018/restoring-trust-in-the-wine-industry.

CHAPTER 11

Tokenization

Everything Will Be Tokenized

Blockchains are basically made for buying, selling, and transacting around digital asset tokens. Bitcoin is the "OG" token. And the great breakthrough of Ethereum was the idea that you could define tokens and then write programs that allow those tokens to operate with a high degree of automation. The result was first an explosion of many different tokens (during the so-called "ICO boom" of 2017 and 2018) then an explosion in ways for them to interact.

In retrospect, it makes sense that decentralized finance (DeFi) and cryptocurrencies were the foundations of the first blockchain bubbles. Cryptocurrencies are easy to create on Ethereum and programmability enables you to do all kinds of nifty things with them, like borrow, transfer, and pay interest. And, best of all, since these assets exist on-chain only, there's no complexity involved in linking a digital asset token to something that exists in the real world.

Tokenization is the single most important thing enterprises can do in the blockchain space. And it's often the first decision that firms make, usually by choosing to notarize documents instead digitize an asset. Document notarization (see that chapter) can be a useful method of tamper-resistance and public accountability, but it's of very little use. In the end, people buy and sell products and assets, not documents.

Tokens have some enormous advantages over documents. The most important is that blockchains apply controls to when and how tokens are created and moved that are very similar to how banks treat money. The global banking system is built upon checks and verifications that are designed to prevent people from losing track of their money.

Even as money has been digitized, it's not easy (very hard in fact) to just hack into a bank and "create" money in your account. It has to come from somewhere. By contrast, in the world of ERP and manufacturing or retail, it's relatively easy to create, add, and remove inventory and assets from enterprise systems. If company A sells a used tractor to company B, they may or may not remove it from their asset list. Since the asset management systems between two companies are not linked, it's impossible to know for sure if the total number of tractors in various companies has gone up or down.

This lack of integration and discipline isn't some kind of massive failure of insight and vision: it's a pragmatic response to the cost and value of keeping track of such things. Historically, tallying money has been, by definition, valuable. For everything else: it depends. Companies didn't integrate their systems because it is extraordinarily expensive to do so and the value proposition was limited.

As the cost of computing and integration goes down and the value proposition of tracking assets goes up, the business case for tokenizing and tracking just about everything starts to emerge. Whether it is building a business on service contracts for products that are out of warranty or keeping track of everything you make, so you can find it and recycle it at end-of-life, the need to tokenize and manage all those assets starts to look inevitable.

Critical Token Types

There are literally hundreds of different token standards and definitions in the Ethereum ecosystem, but there are really only two types that matter: fungible and non-fungible. Everything else is a variation on these two foundational types. You will often hear tokens referred to as "ERC-XXX" where XXX is a number. ERC stands for Ethereum Request for Comment, the process within the Ethereum ecosystem for setting up and defining standards.

The most common and critical token types you will encounter are ERC-20, the standard fungible token, and ERC-721, the standard for non-fungible tokens (NFTs). Fungible tokens are like money: you don't care which token you have, just how many. Non-fungible tokens are unique, though they can be grouped into series. I always remember the difference by keeping in mind that my kids are non-fungible. When I go to school to pick them up, I want my two kids, not any two kids.

The ERC-721 standard was defined back in 2017 with support from Dapper Labs, the Canadian company behind the CryptoKitties online game that generated unique collectible cats. At one point, the trading and sale of Cyrptokitties was so intense, it congested the entire Ethereum blockchain.

There is a third type of token, the ERC-1155, which is gaining traction among enterprise users that represents a blend of fungible and non-fungible token properties. These are useful for building large volumes of tokens that share most common characteristics, but differ based on things like serial numbers. Think of millions of packages of medicine or smartphones coming off a production line. The attraction of the 1155 standard is that these tokens can be handled in large batches with low transaction fees, which is preferable for enterprise users.

The 1155 standard has a few other interesting features including the ability to mint a token as a fungible token and then, once the token is redeemed by the first owner, to become non-fungible. This is a great way to keep track of items that are the same at the time of production. But, once purchased, they may become unique based on how they are used. ERC-1155s also have a "safe transfer" function that allows the original sender to recall them if they are transferred incorrectly (unlike most other digital assets which go only one way).

Today, the vast majority of tokens out there are fungible tokens; non-fungible and other types of tokens represent just a small segment of the total Ethereum ecosystem. Over time, I think that imbalance will start to change as firms tokenize assets. The volumes are likely to be enormous as industrial applications take hold. We have one client that wants to tokenize 500,000 items a day coming off their production lines.

Endless Variability

One of the things that makes Ethereum and digital tokens more useful than Bitcoin or traditional financial applications is that you can define just about anything about how a token operates with smart contracts. All tokens are defined through a smart contract and you can, in the process of definition, open up control of how those tokens are created, transferred, and used.

The process of defining tokens through smart contracts opens some very interesting possibilities for enterprises and business ecosystems. Businesses can control the operation of tokens in ways that copy how you operate in the real world. For example, if you operate a licensing system, you can create smart contracts that allow your business partners to mint additional tokens.

You can also do things such as create linked tokens where one represents the legal ownership or an asset and the other represents the physical item. In the real world, these are often separate (think of the logistics company transferring an asset – they have it in their possession, but they don't own it). And so if we are on a path to building a digital "twin" of our business operations in the blockchain, we need to do the same.

Case Example: Fungible ERC-20 Tokens, The AAVE Governance Token

AAVE is an open-source liquidity protocol, which is a fancy way of saying that it's a DeFi service that allows you to earn income by depositing your assets into the network, or to borrow against your assets as collateral. It's one of the earliest in this space and among the most successful, with about $7 billion in assets across five different chains.

AAVE has a governance token which is a fungible ERC-20 token that allows AAVE token owners to vote on the control of the ecosystem and proposals for adjusting the governance approach and operations. The AAVE governance token, in theory, could eventually resemble a stock share in a company, allowing owners of the ecosystem to earn dividends from the ecosystem transaction fees and profits or the token. The token could increase in value through token buy-backs and "burns" which remove tokens from the ecosystem, decreasing supply.

Case Example: Cyrptopunk Nonfungible Tokens

CryptoPunks were the first wildly successful non-fungible art-focused tokens to be offered. CryptoPunks are a collection of 10,000 generated characters. Punks are differentiated based on things like gender, skin color, accessories, hair types and more. Each one is unique as part of the series and is considered the first real inspiration for both the NFT art craze and the ERC-721 standard on which nearly all NFTs are built.

Even though it is easy to copy the underlying art of a CryptoPunk, the real attraction for many came from the unique and provable digital ownership model. Thanks to controls built into the smart contract, only one person can own a CryptoPunk at a time and those rules are set and enforced by the smart contract.

Case Example: Pharmaceutical ERC-1155 Tokens

While ERC-20 tokens are all the same and ERC-721s are all unique, there is a middle ground where most enterprises exist: where they make large volumes of similar, if not identical, products but need to track them individually. In the case of an EY client in the pharmaceutical industry, they are using 1155 tokens to track packages of medicine that are serialized.

Medicines are often made in batches and regulators require pharmaceutical companies to be able to track and recall batches of medicine if there's contamination or some other problem. Using the 1155 standard, this firm can mint large volumes of tokens and transfer them in big batches to distributors and others.

Right now, this work is all confidential and confined to a private blockchain. Until recently, the public Ethereum lacked robust privacy systems. As privacy matures, it will be possible to migrate this solution onto public Ethereum and then scale it up.

Real World Assets, Future Path & Implementation Considerations

To-date, most of the items that have been tokenized on-chain start and exist entirely on-chain. This is the easiest type of digital asset to handle because no external connectivity is required. However, given that the vast majority of the world's assets exist outside of the blockchain ecosystem, that's not a sustainable path forward.

The future of most enterprise tokens is one where we are modeling and managing assets, real or digital, that exist off-chain. For these, we need connectivity to real world systems that keep the status of these updated and synchronized with the on-chain model. This is so important; I've devoted an entire chapter to the process of integrating off-chain data into on-chain activity.

As for enterprise assets, the future is mostly non-fungible. Money is fungible but much of what is built in the world today is non-fungible or semi-fungible. The more valuable something is, the more likely it is to be non-fungible in nature. Real estate, cars, buildings, and other major assets, even when they start out as identical, end up as unique, non-fungible items.

If there is a big downside for enterprise users, it is that non-fungible items are easy to track on a blockchain. While fungible items can be mixed and moved through exchanges and held by custodians, non-fungible items are easy to track in the current environment. As privacy technology matures, that will change and the real "tokenization of everything" (long a holy grail for people in blockchain tech) will begin.

Implementation Considerations

1. What are you tokenizing?
    a. Is it fungible, non-fungible, or semi-fungible?
2. Why are you tokenizing it?
    a. Product traceability
    b. Ownership tracking
    c. Warranty management
    d. Asset to be sold
    e. Recycling / circular economy
3. Is this a real world asset or is it digital but not on-chain?
    a. How will you keep maintain the synchronization between on-chain and off-chain?
    b. What will you do when that is no longer possible?
    c. How long does that link need to be maintained in order to satisfy the business case?

4.   What are the constraints that should be used to define the asset?
      a.   Who can mint it
      b.   Who can transfer it
      c.   Do you expect the asset to change over time?
      d.   Does the asset have a deliberately designed limited-time life?
5.   Does the asset really need more than one token?
      a.   Do you need to separate ownership from the physical asset?
      b.   Can this asset be leased? Would you tokenize the lease?
      c.   Would someone want to borrow against the value of this asset? If so, how would that affect your design approach
6.   What are the privacy requirements around this asset?
      a.   Do you care if your competition can see it?
      b.   Do you want your customers to be able to demonstrate (or brag!) about their ownership of the asset?
      c.   Does provenance or ownership history of the asset increase its value?

BIBLIOGRAPHY

Cheng, Deric. "Your Guide to ERC-1155: Comparing ERC-721 to ERC-1155." *Alchemy* (blog), November 17, 2021. https://medium.com/alchemy-api/your-guide-to-erc-1155-comparing-erc-721-to-erc-1155-cbf624a34657.

CHAPTER 12

The Grand Unified Theory of Blockchain Business Process Management

If there is a single sentence summarizing how I believe blockchains will transform the world of enterprise computing, it is this: Blockchains will do for business ecosystems what ERP did inside the single enterprise.

To unpack this, understand how it will change the world of enterprise computing, it is worth taking time to understand how ERP transformed business, and the limits ERP faces as companies and business models evolve.

Enterprises, MRP, ERP and Scale

The history of the world's largest companies is one of achieving ever larger-scale. A century ago, the largest companies in the world had as many as 50,000 employees. Standard Oil, one of the largest companies in the U.S. in the 1920s, had 25,000 employees in 1925. That seems like a big number, but in fact, it pales in comparison to the largest companies today. Wal-Mart and Amazon each employ well over one million workers each, and at peak times in the holiday season, Wal-Mart has over two million workers.

U.S. Steel produced revenues of $1.4 billion in 1925, worth roughly $24 billion today, adjusting for inflation. In today's dollars, U.S. GDP in 1925 was $850 billion, which means that U.S. Steel represented 0.16% of that year's national output. By contrast, Wal-Mart had revenues of $559 billion in 2020, representing 2.8% of U.S. GDP that year. By many different measures, the biggest companies today are much bigger than the largest companies a century ago.

What makes big companies bigger? A significant factor is certainly the maturing of physical infrastructure. The late-1800s and early-1900s were a time of enormous infrastructure development in the world's leading industrial countries like the U.S. and the U.K. Thousands of miles of roads and railroads were laid down, enabling national and global supply chains to scale up.

By the 1920s, however, the pace of physical infrastructure building had slowed somewhat, especially railroad building in the United States. The country was covered from coast-to-coast. What did change, starting in the 1920s and continuing on for decades, was a massive build-up in information technology. It was the rise of enterprise computing systems that made standardized processes repeatable at scale on a national and then global level.

Starting in the 1890s and accelerating rapidly, companies started automating accounting using punch cards. Herman Hollerith held key patents on punch-card based tabulating systems and started the Computing-Tabulating-Recording Company in 1911. The firm changed its name in 1924 to International Business Machines (IBM).

IBM punch card machines and then IBM mainframes became the foundation for business process standardization and automation around the world. At first, companies started by picking off unique elements of the business process that could be digitized: initially accounting, then utility bills and consumption. Over time, these process elements became bigger and bigger, including airline reservations systems or manufacturing planning.

The concept of Manufacturing Requirements Planning (MRP) was pioneered by General Electric and Rolls-Royce in the 1950s, and then industrialized and first used commercially by Black+Decker in 1964. From simple estimates of manufacturing supplies needed, MRP gradually evolved into ERP – Enterprise Resource Planning – and this started to subsume all the prior components of computerized business activity into a single set of integrated systems. In the world of ERP, manufacturing was planned, supplies ordered, products made, put into inventory, and then sold, with every transaction linked and tracked into a single integrated picture for finance and operations.

Standardized digital systems made it possible for companies to implement and scale up standardized processes around the world. Large companies, in turn, could serve each other at scale across the country and later across the world. Simple things that were impossible to enforce in the past, like global purchasing agreements, suddenly became feasible as companies could track spending by category, set preferred suppliers, and track down unauthorized deviations from policy. Distance from headquarters stopped being a pass to breaking enterprise policies.

Rise of the Network Enterprise

The business of implementing ERP systems became the single biggest part of the enterprise information technology sector. SAP, based in Germany, is often credited as the first company to fully build out the concept of ERP with the release of R2 in 1979. By 1982, more than 250 companies had deployed SAP's

ERP software and, by 1988, that number had risen to 1,000. Oracle and Microsoft also run significant ERP businesses serving medium and large size enterprises.

But by the 1990s, it was also becoming clear that the nature of companies was changing, and even as ERP started to become a widely deployed tool for managing firms, the scope of the work that needed to be managed was starting to evolve. Companies were moving away from operating as more vertically-integrated organizations to ones that depended more and more on suppliers and business partners as integral parts of their operations.

Today, the world's biggest companies are more like digital ecosystems. Apple and Google both bring mobile phones to market, but both firms are really hubs in a vast system that depends heavily on key partners for innovation, technology, supplies and distribution. As these ecosystems become more complex, the value proposition of ERP starts to diminish. ERP is useful for integration operations within an enterprise, but the ability to monitor, manage, and control activity goes away when enterprises start to depend on other firms.

Once you cross company boundaries, many of the things that ERP systems sought to standardize, monitor, and control, become hard to manage. Inventory and procurement are good examples. Inside a firm, inventory can be managed very tightly. Completed items off the production line can be moved into warehouses and then sent to a shipping partner. Fully-integrated internal systems make sure that when a product is sent from the production area to the warehouse, the inventory in the production system is decreased by one, and the inventory in the warehouse is increased.

The same operational discipline doesn't necessarily happen once you cross company boundaries. There are few automated systems for reconciliation that make sure that a distributor deletes items sent to a shipping carrier, or that data about things like serial numbers and production dates are maintained as the item moves across the network. The result is decreasing accuracy and visibility in process performance.

Metcalf's Law, EDI, Web Portals and Future Monopolists

Companies try to maintain both accuracy and visibility across boundaries, but the tools available to do so are limited and have significant shortcomings. The most widespread tool in use today is EDI – Electronic Data Interchange.

EDI, which dates from the 1970s, is a form of Business-to-Business text messaging. The arrival of EDI enabled companies to standardize how they interact with each other. EDI messages are standardized and administered by the United Nations Economic Commission for Europe. The system originated with the need for automation at scale with air cargo and was first implemented at

Heathrow Airport in 1971. Since then, it has become the global standard for Business to Business integration, particularly in manufacturing. Nearly all ERP systems can handle the input and output of standardized EDI messages.

A quick look at some of the standardized messages shows how much enterprise commerce is covered:

EDI ID	Message	Purpose
850	Purchase Order	Transmit a purchase order from a buyer to a supplier including quantity and agreed upon prices
810	Invoice	Transit the amount owed for products, services, shipped under a purchase order
856	Advance Shipping Notice	Shipment information such as items, tracking numbers and estimated arrival dates.
997	Functional Acknowledgement	Confirmation of EDI message receipt
855	Purchase Order Acknowledgement	Confirmation of PO receipt, including the ability to confirm (or refuse) requested product volumes

EDI was a transformation because it allowed for the transmission of structured business information between companies. In effect, ERP systems could be extended beyond enterprise boundaries to coordinate work at suppliers and distributors without manually re-entering all the necessary information.

Though it was a big step forward for the time, EDI falls far short of the ideal when we look at the available technology choices today. From the beginning EDI has suffered from three major shortcomings:

- EDI messages are point-to-point messages, so data ends up pooling in islands and information tends to only flow one stop up or down the supply chain, even though critical dependencies are often more than one stop away.

- EDI messages contain only information from one party in a transaction to another, not business logic, and they don't necessarily represent the agreement between two firms. The buyer may be entitled to a volume discount that isn't reflected in the purchase order price or the invoice.

- EDI messages do not stop information from being replicated or re-entered (and lost) up and down the supply chain and they do require reconciliation between parties. For example, if a shipment notice sent via EDI does not necessarily mean that the supplier's inventory system has decreased availability by the amount sent and a receipt confirmation does not necessarily do the same at the buyer's location.

- Without continuous reconciliation, errors accumulate in the system's data. Data errors also accumulate as different IT systems constantly receive, re-build, and then propagate information onwards. Little things like the original serial number at a supplier may or may not get passed along down the line. But they become critical information when you need to find a bad batch of lettuce or medication ingredients or malfunctioning batteries.

All of these problems are easily solved by moving from point-to-point messaging to a shared supply chain information system. Web-based portals make this possible. Companies can and do create shared online databases that allow for both continuous updates to inventory information as it moves across the network. They can also apply shared business rules like volume discounts or automatic replenishment plans.

Web-based portals have gained some traction, particularly with very large companies, but they too typically suffer from ingrained problems. Either they are too proprietary to a single enterprise, or they pose a strategic threat to the security of their enterprise users. Big companies that set up their own proprietary supply chain networks all suffer from this first problem: a supply chain system that's optimized for a single big mobile phone or PC maker probably doesn't necessarily work well for automotive suppliers.

These types of company centric solutions work well if you're a giant industry leader and have the power to coerce your suppliers and partners to join this network and spend the money required to build customized interfaces from the member firms' ERP systems.

The alternative approach is an industry or general-purpose web portal for B2B transactions. These are general purpose enough to serve all companies, but thanks to Metcalfe's Law, they represent a strategic threat to the long-term security of all their users because they are future digital monopolists.

Metcalfe's Law states that the value of a telecommunications network is proportional to the square of the number of connected users of the system. While this was initially only intended to apply to Ethernet, it turns out this is a pretty good guess at how just about any commercial or digital network will evolve.

In the case of Ethernet, this turns out to be a pretty harmless, public, open standard for connecting up computers. When it comes to commerce, and you're talking about a single company that is connecting up firms or consumers, what you are talking about is a path towards monopoly control of a business environment.

The number of industries in which this has happened is astonishing. We can see the process at work with desktop operating systems, mobile operating systems, consumer web auctions, ride-sharing, apartment sharing and vacation rentals, and even social networks. Over and over again, single dominant players emerge in every network-based digital service environment.

At first, the emergence of these digital networks is a boon for connecting buyers and sellers and integrating complex business processes. Think about how much more efficient mobile-based ride-hailing is compared to the taxi-dispatch process of old. In the old process, you called for a cab, which was dispatched by radio. After the cab arrives, you paid in cash or by credit card. Nearly every stop in this process is run in a separate system and pieced together manually.

By contrast, in a mobile-based ride-sharing environment, the entire experience is handled in a single, integrated digital system. Dispatch, transport, payment and process monitoring is all handled in a single solution. Not only are all parts of the transaction automatically reconciled with each other, but bad drivers (and riders) get held accountable for their performance. The first time I used a ride-sharing service and just walked away without handling any paperwork for the bill felt like magic.

As wonderful as these fully integrated web portals are for matching buyers and sellers, they are as deadly to B2B companies as they are to consumer taxi services. The natural consequence of any of these services is that they end up as digital monopolies. And once these monopolies become dominant, their operating model shifts from connecting buyers and sellers to exploiting buyers and sellers.

While consumers may click on "accept" and proceed, enterprise buyers have demonstrated they are reluctant to go down the path of using these integrated B2B portals precisely because they know how these "two-sided" business models invariably evolve as time goes on. I believe this explains why we have never seen an Amazon or an Uber-like company come to dominate the B2B side of a particular industry ecosystem.

Efforts to set up industry portals that could monetize and exploit matching buyers and sellers were big in the early 2000s and efforts were attempted again in the early years of "enterprise" blockchain. In both cases, wary enterprise buyers limited the output of these efforts to little more than standards bodies and clearinghouses for EDI information. There is little enthusiasm for shifting away from a flawed but open system like EDI to one that may be much better, but brings risks down the road.

Money for Stuff, Under Agreed-Upon Terms

The dominance of EDI as the world's preferred B2B integration standard, nearly 50 years after it first emerged, is a testament to how much risk enterprise users see in web-based centralized alternatives. The arrival of public block-chains with enabling privacy technologies finally offers an alternative that combines the best capabilities of web portals – unified data and shared business logic – with truly open standards. The decentralized nature of public Ethereum means that, like the internet, the blockchain may become a de-facto monopoly, but it's not one that will end up turning exploitive.

When you boil down nearly every B2B transaction, they all largely have the same core components: buyer and seller are exchanging money for stuff under the terms of an agreement. Highly liquid financial markets don't typically need the agreement part – they are often just executing direct swaps. Between companies, agreements are often essential. Most long-term business relationships need a set of rules and governance for payment, volume discounts and handling disputes.

With Ethereum, it's possible to represent the money and the stuff (real or virtual) as digital tokens, and to convert the key terms of the agreement into a smart contract. The result is the ability to capture and automate most B2B transactions. This works extremely well in supply chain management, but you can apply similar models to just about any other business. From real estate to insurance to investing, the principles are similar – the exchange of money for a product or service, even if that service is not tangible, such as insurance.

The Real Blockchain Enterprise Value Proposition

In the early days of public blockchains, we tended to focus too much on the extreme ability of blockchain technology to turn everything into a speculative financial market. Even when discussing supply chain management, it often seems like the purpose of tokenizing inventory or receivables is to create a financial market for them.

I think that automation and integration may prove to be the most enduring value proposition for blockchain technology. Though payments and access to finance will be useful, it is integration and automation that is often the most complex and expensive part of an on-going B2B relationship.

When crypto-boosters tend to get starry-eyed talking about a payments revolution, I think they are missing the point. In a B2B relationship, the payments are actually one of the lowest-cost and least complex elements of the relationship.

Take something like a long-term supply agreement for a manufacturing company. The buyer has integrated key components from the supplier into their product. This means they are dependent on that supplier and they are working together for the long-term. In turn, that means each individual transaction is, in and of itself, just one part of a bigger whole relationship. Usually, this means sellers offer buyers special consideration such as standardized pricing, volume discounts, and guaranteed service levels with penalties.

When a purchase order goes from a buyer to a supplier, it is the start of a multi-step fulfillment process. When the invoice finally returns, usually with the shipped products, the payment needs to be made. But the real cost of administering the agreement isn't in the payment. It's in all the verification that has to happen along the way:

- Did the original purchase order comply with the terms of the agreement (advance notice, etc)?
- Did the supplier provide the requested items on time? Did they all pass quality checks?
- Does the invoice correctly account for agreed upon payment terms and volume discounts or rebates?

Reconciling and verifying this information across multiple systems is costly. Sending payment is cheap. It's often estimated that, on average, large companies spend around $100 in administrative costs, for each payment processed. That dwarfs the actual cost of the payment.

ERP solved very similar problems inside the enterprise: it took processes and operations that were difficult to standardize and verify and made them uniform. It united inside a single system the business processes that should be integrated automatically, like converting new customer orders into expanded supply requirements.

Public blockchains, meaning really public Ethereum, will offer very similar capabilities, but with the ability to transcend enterprise boundaries. It will truly do for networks of companies what ERP did inside the enterprise.

At the end of this book, I will come back to this question and discuss how far this might go and what we should expect as these capabilities emerge.

DATA SOURCES:

AT&T. "A Brief History: The Bell System," 2008.
   https://web.archive.org/web/20080906194409/http://www.att.com/history/history3.html.
A., Julija. "Fortunly's Annotated Guide to a Century of US GDP by Year." Reference Data,
   December 16, 2022. https://fortunly.com/statistics/us-gdp-by-year-guide/.
Da Cruz, Frank. "Early Card Punch Machines." Columbia University Computing History,
   September 28, 2007. http://www.columbia.edu/cu/computinghistory/oldpunch.html.

"History of Ford Motor Company." In *Wikipedia*, December 22, 2022.
https://en.wikipedia.org/wiki/History_of_Ford_Motor_Company.

IBM Corporation. "The IBM Punched Card." Accessed January 29, 2023.
https://www.ibm.com/ibm/history/ibm100/us/en/icons/punchcard/.

UNECE Sustainable Development. "Introducing UN/EDIFACT." Accessed January 29, 2023.
https://unece.org/trade/uncefact/introducing-unedifact.

Kauflin, Jeff. "America's Top 50 Companies 1917-2017." *Forbes*, September 17, 2017.
https://www.forbes.com/sites/jeffkauflin/2017/09/19/americas-top-50-companies-1917-
2017/?sh=7610ed916295.

"Material Requirements Planning (MRP)," December 18, 2022.
https://corporatefinanceinstitute.com/resources/valuation/material-requirements-
planning-mrp/.

Planes, Alex. "A History of Ridiculously Big Companies." *The Motley Fool* (blog), October 1, 2018.
https://www.fool.com/investing/general/2012/08/22/a-history-of-ridiculously-big-
companies.aspx.

Simmonds, Jon. "SAP's History – Fifty Years and Counting." *ERP Today* (blog), 2021.
https://erp.today/fifty-years-and-counting/.

New York Times. "US Steel Gain $5,000,000 in Net." March 22, 1926.
https://timesmachine.nytimes.com/timesmachine/1926/03/22/98466764.pdf?pdf_redirect=
true&ip=0.

Watzinger, Martin, and Thomas Fackler. "How Antitrust Enforcement Can Spur Innovation: Bell
Labs and the 1956 Consent Decree." *American Economic Journal* 12, no. 4 (2020).
https://pubs.aeaweb.org/doi/pdfplus/10.1257/pol.20190086.

CHAPTER 13

Product & Asset Traceability

Does it matter where your beer came from? The answer, for many people, is "yes." Product traceability has been one of the most popular and enduring applications of blockchain technology in the enterprise space. And in this chapter, I will look at how these applications work, some specific case studies, and why they have proven to be so popular and enduring with enterprise users.

Value Proposition

I think that product traceability has emerged as one of the first and best use cases for enterprises on Ethereum because it creates real, if rather limited value. It is simple to implement, and, provided firms are careful to differentiate between batches and sources of products and actual volumes, it can be done in full public view without disclosing sensitive business information.

For most consumer products, the value proposition around traceability is in the prevention of fraud and verification of sources. In some markets, like India and China, consumers are especially sensitive to the risk of product counterfeiting and so each additional form of verification adds value to the product.

For many other markets, product traceability provides additional authenticity and an ability for consumers to trace the history of a product. There are anecdotal case studies that show incremental margin on verifiably organic products, for example.

The case for traceability gets firmer as you delve into products like pharmaceuticals for which counterfeiting are potentially life-and-death issues. In these cases, the ability to trace bad batches of ingredients down through the supply chain quickly is invaluable. Traceability has some limitations, however, for maintaining enterprise confidentiality.

One of the most valuable features of blockchain technology for a traceability use case is the continuity and linkage of information across enterprise boundaries. Today, many companies do an excellent job of tracking supply and output inside their four walls, but they do not find it easy to match up supply data from one end of the supply chain to another. It's not that the data doesn't exist, but rather that it exists in digital silos. The more times it gets re-entered as it moves from one company to another, the more likely it is to be entered incorrectly or incorrectly matched with the corresponding output product. On the blockchain, tokens move through the ecosystem as they get integrated into products without data re-entry.

Case Study: Peroni Beer

Peroni Nastro Azzurro (Asahi Company), the Italian brewery, is one of the world's biggest users of blockchain traceability technology. Nearly every bottle of beer they make and sell worldwide now features a QR code for product traceability, usually located near the neck of the bottle and close to the serial number printed from the production system.

The main audience for this solution is consumers, who are growing increasingly interested in product sourcing information. Peroni wanted to be able to show people the source of the beer ingredients and the journey from farm to bottle. The firm had a secondary objective which was to start gathering more granular product sustainability data along the way including sourcing and biodiversity data.

In deciding to start sharing production data, Peroni had to face a couple of specific challenges that are common to companies going down this path.

First, it had to structure their information in a way that provided some transparency without sharing sensitive business information. Peroni ultimately selected batch information. Batches of beer are made from common sets of ingredients but vary enormously in size. A single batch of beer may make its way into several slightly different products that share the same content, as defined by packaging and other factors.

The second problem is how to mark and package the output. Unlike many of the previous traceability efforts on higher end items like wines and pharmaceuticals, beer is a low-cost product produced in high volume. It's not practical to spend any significant amount of money on unique labels or individual blockchain tokens. Indeed, on a one-token per bottle, Peroni could absorb much of the world's blockchain capacity by themselves.

The solution for Peroni was to set up one token per batch and then allow end users to put in the serial number on the bottle to locate the detailed source data for that product. The QR code on each bottle takes users to a standardized landing page, from there, entering the serial number retrieves the batch data. The batch data page, in turn, has a link to the relevant blockchain transactions that can be viewed on Polygon Scan for verification. This keeps total costs much lower than trying to create customized QR codes on each bottle.

Underlying each batch NFT, Peroni worked with their suppliers to set up a customized data upload process. This extends across more than 500 farmers, 1 malt house, and 3 brewery plants. Once batch standards were defined, Peroni obtained cooperation from malt houses and farmers to start feeding the data. Each participant is responsible for packaging their own data, either through a CSV file or directly from the company's ERP system. Those looking at a beer NFT from Peroni on the Polygon PoS chain (an Ethereum side chain), will be able to see Peroni's final batch token as well as input tokens from the malt house and the farms.

With a specific batch of beer, f you can follow the beer back to the farm source:

The transaction hash is on the Polygon Proof of Stake Network:

(The full URLs for the Peroni links are in the bibliography, but I created shortened links here in case you're reading the paper copy of the book – they should be much easier to type in if you want to verify yourself.)

Transaction hash:
0xf9d5c4b5bca87788b1b853a53a045a2aa6811e958978817fa0bfd4e11 09c9e77
Peroni's Link: https://tinyurl.com/29y3kbbc
PolygonScan Link: https://tinyurl.com/3k5pmejs

This batch of beer contains malt from multiple batches, including batch 2366 and was completed on 6th of February 2023.

The malt batch that included batch 2366 was finished on 30 November 2022. There are in fact many batches of gain that were mixed together into this large batch:

Transaction hash:
0x491c4a4eb28cc7019e2866afa2ca9ee80d5046885bad7ceaffc20eeba8 3df059
Peroni's Link: https://tinyurl.com/2p9etha4
PolygonScan Link: https://tinyurl.com/4z55nk7m

This batch of malt, in turn, was made from many sources of grain, including the one identified as "09C08082022" where harvesting was completed and the grains were brought together on 30 November 2022:

Transaction hash:
0x8badeaf8e0d7202dd2e0eda6183ecd0eed220e2e41ccc1afaa910bbe-
afa022d1
Peroni's Link: https://tinyurl.com/4hhjats9
PolygonScan Link: https://tinyurl.com/etjfz68k

Each firm in the supply chain is separately responsible for gathering their own data. The raw data is then submitted through EY's OpsChain application, which matches up batch information with the data model and mints production NFTs. Each firm has their on-chain wallet, so you can see how tokens move between wallets as well, for example.

One thing that is missing from the overall solution is the independent verification of the source data. While the blockchain makes it impossible for data to be altered after the fact, there is no external process yet verifying the correctness of the original data.

Another thing you will notice if you go through the data set is that it's not possible to verify the total volume of beer, malt or grain. Not much is specified about the batches and sources. This is deliberate – it means that Peroni can track bad batches of grain or malt and customers can see the origin of their products, but competitors cannot ascertain business volume or performance information.

From a marketing standpoint, the investment has been a huge success and from a technology standpoint, the foundation has been laid with infrastructure and suppliers for a long-term sustainability data collection and verification strategy.

Peroni's longer-term goal is to implement a full trusted-data ecosystem and to start using privacy technology and smart contracts to automate supply chain operations. This is just their first step along the way.

Case Study: Takeda Plasma Traceability

Medicines, known as Plasma-Derived Therapies, are used in treatments for an astonishing array of different diseases. Many of them are rare diseases where components of blood from healthy patients are used to supplement or replace missing or damaged parts of patient blood. The demand for plasma and related therapies far exceeds the supply and the supply chain itself is fragile.

Plasma is the main component of blood that is used to create many of these therapies. It represents about 55% of a typical liter of blood, though only 15% of that is usable protein. The rest is mostly water. Turning this plasma into medicine is another enormous challenge. Bio-pharmaceutical facilities are themselves very complex and can often cost upwards of $1 billion to build and start-up.

The supply chain itself for plasma is also enormously complex. It starts with individuals who must donate plasma. From there, it must be frozen, transported, thawed, and then combined with other donations into the manufacturing process. It takes about 70,000 individual donations to make one batch of several hundred therapies, it is a complex many-to-many mapping of starting materials to finished products. Individual donors are themselves highly variable. Some people have antibodies in their plasma that are much more useful or more highly concentrated than others. It also takes about three weeks to recover from donating, which means that donation frequency and other lifestyle factors play a major role in the quality of plasma collected.

The industry has grown up slowly over decades as the space has matured, with multiple different companies involved, from collecting plasma at retail locations to shipping, tracking plasma and distributing finished products. The result is that the industry suffers from significant information gaps between firms even as regulators require more and more precise tracking of outputs.

Takeda Pharmaceuticals is one of the largest plasma-derived therapies manufacturers in the world. Though their Biolife division they operate a network of plasma collection centers in addition to sourcing plasma from other established entities (i.e., the American Red Cross).

Starting in 2020, Takeda embarked on an ambitious project called PlasmaChain to try to connect their plasma supply chain end-to-end. The goal of PlasmaChain was to use tokens and smart contracts to show how individual donations passed through the entire network and on to products themselves. Right now, PlasmaChain operates within Takeda on a private blockchain, tracking individual therapy outputs. The future roadmap calls for implementation of privacy technology and deployment into a public network to connect additional plasma collectors and supply chain partners.

A system the size of Takeda's points to the challenges that industrial companies will face as they scale up traceability operations. Multiple partners are needed, data has to be integrated on-chain in a common format, and privacy solutions have to be executed. And all of this has to be done at a volume that far exceeds what is typically executed each day on Ethereum. While each part of this is possible, nobody has yet combined all these pieces in the way that Takeda's ambitious long-term roadmap implies.

Solution Design, Considerations & Limitations

To date, the theory of product traceability is better than the reality. More often than not, there is no external verification that supports assertions made on-chain about organic sources. Furthermore, companies have been careful to limit the amount of data exposure they have provided. Revealing suppliers and even batch data can start to move from information that's acceptable in a public environment into an area where it is possible to ascertain sensitive business information such as volumes, sources, and changes in demand.

One key element of this process is getting data with high integrity into the blockchain repository. Blockchains are not magical repositories of truth. Instead, they will faithfully preserve data from the original source, so it's important that companies which implement on-chain traceability start with high quality data.

On-chain data for traceability depends upon the reliability of the enterprise putting that data online. Without a third party to review the data process for creating source data and putting it on the blockchain, how can the end customer truly know that it is truthful? To date, I can't think of a single client I have worked with that has implemented an external reporting verification process for its own traceability data.

As stakes shift from marketing activities towards more strategic outputs such as product safety and recalls verification of source data is going to be increasingly important. In those circumstances, it makes sense to consider buying what is known in the audit industry as a SOC report – Systems and Organization Controls report. SOC reports have auditors independently examine aspects of a company's operations and make those reports available externally. This can include assessments of privacy, business process, system integration reliability and data confidentiality. SOC reports come in a variety of "flavors" – SOC1, SOC2, SOC3 depending what is being examined and who is allowed to see the reports. SOC3 reports may be the most valuable in these circumstances as they can be used externally with the general public.

Notwithstanding the limitations presented, however, product traceability is one of the simplest and fastest ways for a company to dip its toe into the world of Ethereum and start issuing tokens.

Future Path

Because traceability is simple to implement and requires a direct connection to supply chain activities, I believe that for many firms, traceability will act as a gateway into more substantial activities as follow-ons:

1. **Anti-counterfeiting initiatives**. As traceability data gets more and more granular, it becomes easier to identify counterfeit products. If your bottle of Italian wine was made in 2015 and sold by a retailer in

China in 2019, you should probably be suspicious of it if you're buying it in Australia in 2022.

2. **Recall management**. Tracing bad ingredients to finished goods can help companies reduce customer risks and warranty costs.

3. **Supply Chain Management**. Once the integration with supply chain systems is done and blockchain privacy systems are available, I expect to see companies start migrating their traceability solutions towards full supply chain management systems.

Product traceability becomes more useful as the level of granularity in the system becomes higher, but at a certain point, the highest value comes with full granularity, and that means switching towards a more privacy-protected model discussed in the chapter on supply chain management.

Implementation Considerations:

Summary of key considerations in implementing a product traceability solution.

1. Intended results, audience, and return on investment
    a. Who is the intended audience for this traceability data? Consumers, intermediaries, distributors or other business partners?
    b. What is the primary objective and likely source of ROI? Is it increased consumer trust and a premium position for the brand? Anti-counterfeiting? Recall, warranty, or product safety management?
2. Supply chain definition
    a. Who is participating in the supply chain that will be traced online? From which suppliers or business partners will you require collaboration?
    b. How many steps in the supply chain are needed to provide the traceability that meets the solution objective?
    c. How much granularity is required from each participant?
3. Source data systems and integration plans
    a. Can you match each step in the supply chain and each business partner with an accurate online data source that can be integrated?
    b. What, if any, external verifications are needed to make this solution credible? What tests will you perform to make sure it is working well? Will you hire an external firm or an audit firm to verify these results and possibly public a SOC report?
4. Privacy and security requirements
    a. What are the privacy requirements around each piece of data you are publishing? If you are publishing data from suppliers, for

example, are you comfortable that your competitors may be able to directly read or indirectly deduce your supply partners? Have you taken adequate steps to blind of conceal the identity of key partners if necessary?

    b.   How much granularity will you release in your product traceability process? Will it be based on batch data which may be difficult to discern, or will it get closer to product-specific or shipment specific data?

5.   Tokenization and On-Chain Data

    a.   Is your product best represented by notarizing a document, creating a fungible token, or creating a non-fungible token that represents a product or batch?

6.   End user access

    a.   How will end users access and easily verify the correct information? Will there be a user-friendly landing page from a QR code, a link to a blockchain explorer, or a transaction number?

    b.   If off-chain data is required, how will this be handled? Will it be on an immutable off-chain data system such as IPFS or on a more traditional access-controlled cloud infrastructure?

BIBLIOGRAPHY:

"Peroni Beer Batch Traceability Document." Peroni through EY OpsChain on Polygon Proof of Stake Network, June 14, 2022.
    https://tracciabilitamalto.peroni.it/blockchain/certificate/0x49b789cf028998eb52301da7d7fc2cb03bca7432172e1c2b3e5dcd459cae2664?brewing=2163R2.

"Peroni Farm Source Traceability Document." Peroni through EY OpsChain on Polygon Proof of Stake Network, May 27, 2022.
    https://tracciabilitamalto.peroni.it/blockchain/certificate/0x75cf99413658366993b76933d85c8e39b9a6d4f4d175d5e7189cbad4d539036e?id_granella=03C24062020,04M17062020,19M16112020,16C27112020,06C20092021,09C04032022,15M04012021,06C23072020,08C08022021,04C01022021,1725092020,14C13072020,08C12112021,02C02112021,5204032022,13M24062020.

"Peroni Malt Processing Traceability Document." Peroni through EY OpsChain on Polygon Proof of Stake Network, May 31, 2022.
    https://tracciabilitamalto.peroni.it/blockchain/certificate/0xd4128202f5da90757e53419b15cab8b9e4e5c1a3e4c5ede2902baba67fdc2e18?lotto_malto=497,967,969,956,965,970,972,996,985,973,1012,993.

CHAPTER 14

Supply Chain Management

To understand how profoundly blockchains are likely to transform supply chain management, it's worth taking a step back for a moment to understand a bit of supply chain management history. Black+Decker was the first company in the world to implement computerized Materials Requirements Planning (MRP), all the way back in 1964, though other firms such as Rolls-Royce and GE had developed the early concepts in the 1950s.

In its original form, MRP just converted product requirements into supply requirements. Over time, MRP matured, taking into account manufacturing constraints, equipment scheduling, and existing inventories. Combined with forecasting and sales planning, companies became ever more agile at handling changes in supply and demand, all while needing less inventory.

Even as MRP transformed the ability for companies to manage themselves, it made the biggest challenge in supply chain management – managing an ecosystem of partners – even more prominent. No manufacturing plan is worth anything at all if the necessary parts and components don't show up.

In the 1970s, as MRP spread across the manufacturing world, industry leaders started the process of digitizing their interactions with business partners as well, aiming to plug business partners into an extended digital business network. To that end, firms started plugging in Electronic Data Interchange (EDI), a form of business-to-business messaging that originated in the air cargo industry.

EDI standards were set up to enable end-to-end business processes from Request for Quote to notification of shipment and presentation of invoice. When integrated together and deployed at scale, the results were dramatic, not just at individual firms, but at the level measurable to the economy as a whole. In the 1960s and 1970s, most companies kept inventories worth around 4% of their revenues. Between 1980 and 2000, as MRP and EDI became widespread, that rate declined to around 2.5%. Basically, industry today operates on about half the inventory it used to need.

Value Proposition

Despite the enormous progress made with MRP, then ERP, and the integration of EDI, supply chain management remains one of the biggest challenges most companies face, and cooperation between firms is the single biggest part of that work. Inventories are rising again worldwide, and the rapid shifts in demand brought on by COVID lock-downs, fiscal stimulus, inflation, and then recession have exposed the weaknesses of the EDI-based system.

Supply chains are multi-company ecosystems, but EDI is a point-to-point messaging system. This means islands of data. Additionally, an EDI and MRP world is a world where every firm maintains their own data and process. That means that each firm aims to have a complete (or largely complete) record of the supply chain network inside its own four walls, a truly herculean task which no firm can realistically achieve.

Blockchain technology offers a radically better way to manage an end-to-end supply chain using standardized digital tokens and smart contracts. Just start with the progression of materials through a supply chain. In a traditional discrete manufacturing process, components move from supplier to assembler, which integrates then, and then perhaps on to another entity that completes final assembly before going into product distribution. Each one of those components can be represented either as a fungible token or a non-fungible token.

To illustrate, let's follow the key steps in mobile phone assembly. (If you're a mobile phone industry expert, please forgive me for wildly simplifying your business to create this example.) Key components in this supply chain are processors, memory, displays and batteries. Commodity components in the supply chain are capacitors and cases.

Each manufacturer in the chain takes responsibility for generating the tokens that represent the digital assets they manufacture. Commodity components can be represented as fungible tokens and unique serialized assets can be represented as non-fungible tokens (NFTs).

When the LCD display maker has created a screen, it creates a representative token. And, in this case, because it is a serialized high value component, it is an NFT. The NFT goes into the display-maker's wallet and, upon shipment to the assembler, is sent to the assembler's wallet. The beauty of this is that there is no duplication of data across the ecosystem. The LCD display token moves alongside the physical asset. No need to sync or reconcile, just follow the token. The complete phone and all its related tokens, including the NFT for the display, in turn, moves to the wallet of the distributor or buyer next, and all asset movements are automatically reconciled.

Physical supply chains have long lagged behind the banking ecosystem in one particularly critical respect: they are loosely coupled and not systematically reconciled.

In this model, it is possible for every participant in the supply chain to see all the assets. All kinds of use cases are now enabled:

- Vendor Managed Inventory (VMI). Suppliers can monitor the inventories of assets across the network and manage replenishment shipments accordingly.
- Quality, Warranty & Recalls. High failure rates or defective batches can now be traced and managed across the network. Companies should be able to tell where and exactly how many items must be repaired or recalled.
- Extended supply chain planning. With visibility to actual demand from one of the supply chain to another, companies can avoid over-reacting to rising demand as it gets amplified through the network. A 10% increase in actual end customer demand can easily turn into a 100% increase in orders further back in the supply chain when there are constraints, as buyers panic-order and try to lock up supply.
- Supply Chain Risk Management. Mapping the end-to-end supply chain definitively with multiple steps back in the network will help companies get a much firmer grasp on how much risk and dependency there is in their networks. Efforts to insist on redundant suppliers for each critical component don't necessarily work out if both of those suppliers depend on the same one or two suppliers one tier further back in the network.

Introduction to Case Studies

There are no tokenized inventory management systems running today on public blockchains because there are no industrialized privacy systems available. . At the time of writing, EY has signed the first prototype development agreements based on technology developed by our teams, including Nightfall, the ecosystem for private token transfers. But none of these are live or referenceable.

Instead, for the case studies, it's interesting to look at two examples of efforts in supply chain management that are operating with some degree of success but haven't scaled up into widespread industry adoption. They are still providing useful lessons in how value can be created and what next steps could be taken as privacy solutions mature:

Case Study: IBM FoodTrust

IBM Food Trust, launched in 2017, is a blockchain-based platform enabling participants across the food supply chain to track movement of products from farm to table. Participants include some of the largest food ecosystem leaders, including Walmart, to increase transparency, traceability, and efficiencies across food ecosystems.

Globalization has increased the complexity of food networks and supply chains. Creating transparency of how food is grown, processed, transported is difficult across independent legacy systems that cannot "talk" to one another. In addition, regulatory requirements, such as Section 204(d) of the U.S. FDA Food Safety Modernization Act requires food supply chain stakeholders to rapidly identify and remove potentially contaminated food from the market.

The IBM Food Trust platform is designed to increase transparency, efficiency, and trust in the food industry. The platform is built upon Hyperledger Fabric, a private, permissioned blockchain, allowing food ecosystem partners to share data amongst themselves. Block data is added through validation nodes called Trust Anchors that are designated by a Convener, or ecosystem leader.

Smart contracts automate tracking of food products by scanning products at each stage of the supply chain and recorded on the blockchain in the form of a digital certificate. Product information typically includes product ID (GTIN-14), lot/batch codes, purchase orders, and date/time codes (harvesting, processing, shipping, and receiving). Unlike Ethereum, Hyperledger Fabric does not natively support tokenization, so most batch and lot information is time-stamped, and notarized, rather than tokenized.

Walmart began using the Food Trust platform in 2018 to track movement of leafy greens in response to a series of E. coli outbreaks impacting over 200 people in 36 states. Tracking movement of leafy greens from the farm to the store, Walmart was able to reduce time to identify the source of outbreaks from more than a week to mere seconds. IBM notes Walmart's influence as the largest company in the world in 2019 forced adoption of upstream supply chain partners to the Food Trust network to maintain supplier status. Other companies in the industry have been reluctant to join, however, as they fear that the system is largely controlled by IBM and Walmart and operates to their benefit.

Case Study: Mediledger

MediLedger is a blockchain-based platform for the pharmaceutical industry designed to increase the security and efficiency of the drug supply chain. The platform was developed by Chronicled and initial members included pharmaceutical giants Pfizer and Genentech. Since inception in 2019, MediLedger has added several other drug manufacturers as well as the three largest U.S. wholesalers representing over 90% of drug distribution.

The U.S. Drug Supply Chain Security Act (DSCSA), which passed in 2013, requires pharmaceutical companies to track and trace their products from the manufacturer to the point of dispensing. This is to ensure that counterfeit and stolen drugs do not enter the supply chain, and that patients receive safe and effective medications. The MediLedger platform provides a secure and efficient way to accomplish this task by using blockchain technology.

The platform is an Ethereum private, permissioned blockchain, which acts like a distributed database to enable private data sharing across partners. The rules of the network are governed by the network participants, rather than the greater Ethereum community.

Three core features were built into the platform.:

First, smart contracts automate many tasks required to track and trace pharmaceutical products. Each drug is assigned a unique identifier, which is recorded on the blockchain as a digital certificate and used to track the drug as it moves through the supply chain, from the manufacturer to the distributor to the pharmacy. Second, confidential messaging between partners is enabled through leveraging Electronic Product Code Information Services (EPCIS) standards. Third, zk-SNARKS, or zero-knowledge proofs, are offered as an option to further enhance privacy of proprietary business data.

The platform also uses a consensus algorithm to ensure that the information stored on the blockchain is accurate and secure. In 2022, MediLedger announced a partnership with Parity to develop interoperability with other protocols, opening the aperture for additional use cases.

Adoption of the MediLedger platform was largely compliance driven to conform to the DSCSA. While some efficiencies are gained through reduction of manual verification and paperwork between supply chain partners, any financial returns are minimal. However, MediLedger successfully reduces the risk of counterfeit drugs entering the supply chain, therefore increasing patient safety.

Solution Design, Considerations, & Limitations

Blockchain-based supply chain management sounds amazing, in theory. In practice, this space is off to a very slow start for one critical and overwhelming reason: privacy. Information about what companies buy from each other, who they buy and sell to, and what they pay are among the most sensitive business secrets out there. Without reasonable levels of privacy, all of the ideas outlined in this chapter are non-starters.

The need for privacy and the immense strategic value of this information also explains why, despite its many shortcomings, EDI remains the preferred choice today for many large enterprises. Two of the biggest examples, Food-Trust and Mediledger, both operate on private/permissioned chains and have both struggled to gain client adoption. Participants all have the same fear: That the dominant parties or operators in the network will be unable to resist the temptation in the future to set up toll-booths in the network or use network analytics to their own commercial advantage.

The gradual maturing of privacy that is now taking place means that use cases around supply chain management can be unlocked. Using a combination of on-chain token attributes and off-chain data storage with links in the token, every combination of public and private data storage as well as mutable and immutable attributes can be implemented now, including making the token itself private.

Supply chains that can adapt most effectively sooner rather than later are those supply chains that use more fungible assets and those which have lower requirements for privacy are more likely to be successful.

Future Path

As blockchain privacy solutions come online, I believe that we will see a renewed interest by industrial companies in tokenizing their assets and managing them on Ethereum. That will certainly stress the scalability requirements of the network. A quick back-of-envelope I did with my team told us that we would need capacity for four billion transactions a day to accommodate the global automotive industry. While Ethereum can't do that today, it's well within what we would expect from the network within a decade.

One area that I think could be transformational in the future is a fundamental change in how supply chains are managed. Today, we tend to drive supply chains largely in a top-down manner, executing plans and pushing inventory forward to distribution, where it gets pulled as needed to the final consumption location. The system is a combination of push and pull.

Smart contracts, however, might enable a new, much more pull-centric supply chain model where individual inventory locations have their own smart contracts that manage their own supply levels and have the ability to order supply from whichever nearby location is most efficient. In that respect, networks may start to operate closer and closer to a self-organizing, self-managing model.

Implementation Considerations

1. Intended results, audience, and return on investment
   a. Audience
   b. ROI
2. Supply chain definition
   a. Who is participating in the supply chain that will be traced online? From which suppliers or business partners will you require collaboration?
   b. How many steps in the supply chain are needed to provide the traceability that meets the solution objective?
   c. How much granularity is required from each participant?
   d. Fungible vs. non-fungible
   e. Batches, serialization,
3. Source data systems and integration plans
   a. Can you match each step in the supply chain and each business partner with an accurate online data source that can be integrated?
   b. What, if any, external verifications are needed to make this solution credible? What tests will you perform to make sure it is working well? Will you hire an external firm or an audit firm to verify these results and possibly public a SOC report?
4. Privacy and security requirements
   a. What are the privacy requirements around each piece of data you are publishing? If you are publishing data from suppliers, for example, are you comfortable that your competitors may be able to directly read or indirectly deduce your supply partners? Have you taken adequate steps to blind or conceal the identity of key partners if necessary?
   b. How much granularity will you release in your product traceability process? Will it be based on batch data which may be difficult to discern, or will it get closer to product-specific or shipment specific data?
5. Tokenization and On-Chain Data
   a. Is your product best represented by notarizing a document, creating a fungible token, or creating a non-fungible token that represents a product or batch?
6. End user access
   a. How will end users access and easily verify the correct information? Will there be a user-friendly landing page from a QR code, a link to a blockchain explorer, or a transaction number?

b. If off-chain data is required, how will this be handled? Will it be on
    an immutable off-chain data system such as IPFS or on a more tradi-
    tional access-controlled cloud infrastructure?

CHAPTER 15

Procurement & Contract Management

Procurement is the heart of how most enterprises work with one another. And, it is, I believe, the main way in which blockchain will transform the world of business operations. Nearly every product or service in the world is created from raw materials or services procured as part of the product creation process. This is true no matter how far you go back in the supply chain. Even the most basic raw materials that are mined out of the ground need reliable suppliers of mining equipment.

Over the past few decades, procurement has become ever more important in the enterprise model. In the 1950s, the prototypical factory was the Ford Complex at River Rouge in Detroit. It was a highly integrated factory that included a steel works and a glass works. It's only a slight exaggeration to say that dirt went in one side while cars came out the other. In that factory environment, Ford had immense control over much of the value-add to their automobiles and, therefore, the key success factor in Ford's operations was Ford's planning.

By contrast, if any factory can be said to represent the state of the art today, it might be the Foxconn assembly facilities in Shenzhen for the iPhone. This is a factory that doesn't even belong to the company whose products are assembled there. Indeed, not a single thing about the iPhone is manufactured by Apple, even if everything is designed by that firm. Instead, the key success factor in Apple's supply chain (and for that matter nearly every other mobile phone as well) is its ability to coordinate the production and shipment of millions of items from dozens of suppliers.

Ironically, even as the critical dependencies in most industrial supply chains move from internal to external controls, companies have spent billions on tools to optimize internal operations and very little has been done to extend an optimized digital interface across to business partners. Most business contracts are still executed on paper, or digitized paper, and most purchase orders and fulfillment plans are exchanged by spreadsheets, PDF files, faxes, and EDI messages.

The Cost of Procurement & Contract Management

Even though companies depend more and more on external collaboration, there are a number of reasons holding back the maturation of this technology. The most important is that firms have limited power to impose their preferred tools and processes and suppliers and suppliers are reluctant to hand over too much information or control to any one business partner.

Firms rightly fear industry portals offering standardization and integration across business interactions. The network and software-driven nature of these industry portals means they have high potential to become monopolies, as we've seen with their consumer counterparts, where two-sided business models exploit data flows between buyers and sellers. Given those risks, it's no wonder that despite many efforts, B2B procurement portals have had little success beyond non-critical maintenance equipment and office supplies.

Maintaining a more loosely coupled integration with suppliers that is built on spreadsheets, PDF files, and EDI messages comes with a very steep cost. The biggest costs come in three buckets:

1. **Lost value capture.** Companies are much better at negotiating agreements than they are at implementing them. Most procurement agreements involve discounts, standardized price lists, rebates and standardized terms and conditions. And, even though they all tend to be similar, they are also all unique. Many volume discounts and rebates go unused because they are not tracked easily and most ERP systems are not good at handling complex business rules. This problem gets multiplied when firms delegate purchasing authority to key suppliers.

2. **Higher administrative costs.** Firms spend a great deal of time matching invoices to purchase orders, shipments and contract terms. The administrative cost to review, approve, and pay an invoice from a supplier can easily top $100 each time. The administrative costs are vastly greater than the actual cost of executing the payment.

3. **Reduced visibility across the supply chain.** Even though most modern supply chains stretch out across many layers, most companies have only limited visibility to products and supplies as they move through the network – most often just one tier backwards or forwards. Data silos and data re-entry make it hard to see what is actually coming and the status of availability. Lower visibility is best offset with more inventory – and so higher costs.

The Public Blockchain Value Proposition

Public blockchains like Ethereum potentially solve nearly all the most serious problems firms face when handling procurement across enterprises, but without the risks of handing over critical business information to centralized digital portals. The shared nature of a blockchain ledger means that all transactions are automatically reconciled between the parties, and the focus can shift to getting good data in from the start and agreeing upon.

Let's unpack the layers here:

1. **Tokenization of Assets & Payments.** By tokenizing the assets to be exchanged, particularly the raw material and product inputs, we can make it possible to keep the supply chain reconciled end-to-end. This avoids accidentally ending up with double-counted assets when things are moving between buyer and supplier. It also provides continuity of information along the supply chain. Instead of re-entering data about parts, the whole part is moved at each stage of the journey – along with the data related to that part. This lays the foundation to have absolute alignment between supply chain management and finance, since payments and asset ownership become directly linked with inventory controls. Smart contract enforcement of terms and conditions. This is where it becomes possible for firms to drastically reduce the cost of business administration and capture from negotiated procurement agreements. Converting key terms and conditions into smart contracts means that volume discounts, rebates, and other negotiated terms are enforced automatically. It also means that no additional administrative verification is required to check invoices against contract terms – if the product has been received from the supplier, then smart contracts can handle the rest. It's also possible to open these contracts to multiple parties, enabling firms to delegate buying responsibilities to subcontractors without losing their volume discounts.

2. **Multi-layer visibility.** Because digital asset tokens can be programmable and can have data attachments, it becomes possible to allow each owner of an asset or each party through whom an asset has passed to define what information shall be visible to others in the supply chain. This allows for much more accurate demand, or supply, signals across multiple layers in the network and much more reliable execution of recalls.

3. **Resilience from centralization.** This is the least specific and most strategic issue of them all: centralized systems inevitably end up

empowering the digital intermediary. The result: a never-ending stream of cost increases and adjustments that may have little to do with value creation and are mostly about monetizing user data and extracting value from parties in the system. Centralized systems can do everything decentralized systems can, but they can end up exploiting the participating companies.

It's worth repeating that none of this works on public Ethereum without the implementation of privacy technology. For that reason alone, there are no public blockchain-based enterprise procurement systems. The maturing of privacy technology means that this is a situation that I hope will end soon.

Case Example: Microsoft XBOX Software Licensing System

While there are no public blockchain solutions available, there is one useful private blockchain solution prototype that shows what is possible for contract management and procurement: Microsoft's XBOX Video Game Network developed for Microsoft by EY and now maintained by Microsoft.

The original concept was something closer to an industry utility, but the lack of privacy technology ultimately prevented this from being fully executed. The video game industry is a lot like the movie or music business – there is a lengthy and extended value chain between participants in the creation of a video game and the end customer. Product flows to customers and royalties flow back from game sellers to publishers, to developers, and then back to individual actors. Similar to other creative industries, the process can be opaque and very time-consuming. The shift from legacy system to private blockchain produced some truly notable results: a cycle time reduction of more than 99% and a cost reduction of about 40% overall.

Microsoft had several key objectives when they originally started designing the system with EY. The first was to simplify, speed up, and reduce the cost of managing the simple procurement process. Microsoft has more than 30,000 contracts with suppliers to buy video game licenses and sell them onto end customers. Though they all have relatively similar components (depending on the country, the product, and the market) there may be different royalty rates as well as rules on thresholds for rebates and discounts. Obviously, hot properties and big publishers can negotiate more advantageous deals than smaller firms. The end result is a lot of contracts that are similar but not identical.

The second goal was to develop the network into an industry utility and ecosystem. Microsoft is, at least for the XBOX Network, the ultimate source of truth about how many games have been sold. From there, it can not only pay their immediate suppliers, but could conceivably have brought their major

suppliers and partners on who would, in turn, pay out royalties to their participants. Individual actors or licensees would then be able to trace their payments
directly and logically to the original purchase and contract terms.

Having a single source of truth shared along the value chain should com-
press cycle time and eliminate a lot of errors and cost as well. As of right now,
each firm effectively enters and re-enters data about spend and agreement rules
along the chain.

In the end, only the first phase of this project was completed, as the lack
of privacy technology meant that moving to a public network or inviting other
participants in would expose the details of Microsoft's confidential business
agreements to others. Despite these limitations, however, the project generates
substantial ROI for Microsoft and shows a glimpse of what will be possible as
blockchain privacy matures.

Though the implementation represents some significant complexity in
handling the volume of transactions that Microsoft executes, the high-level
process is relatively straightforward:

- Contracts are ingested into the system and converted to solidity smart
  contracts. We built a customized ML/OCR tool to extract key terms.
  Once the terms are extracted and tested, we send the draft contract to
  both parties for digital signature.
- Once the contracts are in place and signed, we start ingesting the flow
  of transaction data from Microsoft and the smart contract runs on each
  transaction for that client.
- Suppliers can log in at any time to see their outstanding balances or
  check the logic of the contract execution.

In the past, it took Microsoft about 45 days after the conclusion of the
month to complete the statements of account for each video game supplier and
each contract. The challenge was that their existing system could not handle
the full logic of business agreements, so there was a partially automated calcu-
lation followed by a lot of manual adjustments. Shifting to smart contracts
ended all the manual adjustments: up-to-date account statements are available
shortly after transactions are processed. What was 45 days is now down to just
a few minutes.

Product Approach: EY OpsChain Contract Manager

My preference would be to share a case example of a live client using public
Ethereum for their business procurement activities, but at the time of writing
the first edition of this book, no such case examples form EY or any other firm

exist. Nonetheless, it is possible to describe the solution and approach we are building in OpsChain contract manager. The goal with this product is to replicate the overall value proposition of the solution for Microsoft, but in a more general, privacy-enabled approach that can be used on the public Ethereum network.

OpsChain Contract Manager is designed to support the most common enterprise procurement activities initially. Over time, the goal is that just about any B2B contract can be implemented and modeled, though we are still learning how to manage privacy and the interactions between Nightfall and Starlight in a way that minimizes the risk of data leakage. This mainly means implementing price lists, volume discounts and rebates in a smart contract model.

The initial focus is on the automation of pre-existing contracts where the value proposition is around eliminating complex paperwork and administration. As with the Microsoft XBOX approach, existing paper agreements can be converted to smart contracts and then both parties will be able to sign the new digital agreements containing their key requirements.

Buyers will submit purchase orders and sellers will create invoices for products or services that are delivered. It will be optional to create digital tokens to represent those products or services and transfer those as part of the process. Most importantly, those invoices must match the terms & conditions agreed upon in the contract. Payment will be executable in either the blockchain model, through Stablecoins, or through the banking system with the recipient acknowledging payment on-chain.

In the long run, what will most differentiate this blockchain-based approach for procurement from traditional systems is the ability to integrate multiple buyers and sellers into a single contract. If you think about just about any large global firm, a buying group model is more accurate than a single entity. Not only do multi-nationals routinely delegate buying authority to business partners, they also delegate buying authority to national subsidiaries.

The same model is visible on the selling side. Parent companies negotiate global agreements and they expect their national sales subsidiaries or distribution partners to honor those prices and volume purchase agreements. Since very few companies have a single, integrated global ERP, and no companies extend their ERP to sub-contractors, keeping track of enterprise agreements at this global scale isn't possible with traditional ERP-based solutions.

Constraints and Issues

Over the long run, I expect procurement to become one of the main value propositions in the B2B space for blockchain technology. But there are limitations and constraints that need to be considered, especially as we are so early on in the development of this space.

The biggest constraint I foresee comes from the immense complexity of most procurement contracts. Though the core terms of the agreements boil down to a few key things like payment terms, late fees, and forecasting agreements, the contracts often run to dozens of pages. Much of what's in these contracts is subjective language about handling disputes and non-performance, and this cannot be encoded into a smart contract effectively.

Because long-term repeat procurement is known in Game Theory as a "repeat game," the risk of cheating and dishonesty is low. Big companies often work with their main suppliers for decades at a time. While business contracts often contain draconian penalties for non-performance and resolution plans for legal jurisdictions and arbitration, they are almost never invoked. Trying to encode these rules will create several problems.

Blockchains work best with objective data streams. While there are provisions for the concept of external inputs that are subjective, I personally think that we already have an excellent system for dispute resolution that doesn't need re-inventing. More practically, a very large code base for a contract produces a lot of risk from a security standpoint. The more code you have, the harder it is to be confident it is free from bugs and exploits. Since the main value proposition is automation, not dispute resolution, this creates more risk without meaningfully reducing operating costs.

The Path Forward for Procurement

The initial concept for procurement works best in a repeated game model with participants on both sides strongly incentivized to behave well and the objective is automation. Over time, blockchain based contract management can move in three directions: it can handle an ever more sophisticated range of business agreements and it can handle more arms-length types of agreements and it can handle the addition of value-added services based on tokenization.

When it comes to agreement complexity, we are still in the early stages when the goal is to handle buyer and seller agreements with fixed prices, rebates, or volume discounts. Over time we can handle many more buyers and sellers and much more complex business logic. This can include handling large catalogs of prices, exchange rates, fixed and variable logistics costs, and markups and downs by country or service category. Every industry has its particular set of variations or national regulatory rules that will have to be tested and evolve over time.

The second forward path is around a growing ability to handle more arms-length agreements. This would include the bidding process, reputation management, and perhaps a blockchain-based system for proving past delivery to other clients without revealing prices. With these types of functions in place, it should be easier for firms to establish new relationships with confidence.

Finally, I foresee the addition of value-added services based on the tokenization of assets involved in the process – specifically purchase orders, invoices, and inventory assets. There are real-world financial services and logistics services that are already delivered against these things, just not in a fully integrated and digital manner. Companies routinely borrow working capital against purchase orders, factor and sell off invoices, and borrow against inventory assets. All of this could become highly liquid, digital and verified with blockchain-based solutions.

At EY, we often talk about how "blockchain will do for business ecosystems what ERP did inside the enterprise." There is no place where this gets closer to reality than by implementing procurement between firms using a blockchain model. The ability for any company, regardless of size, to integrate the work of another firm quickly and easily into their business model will be transformational. Today, digital integration is the province of large, technically sophisticated firms. In a blockchain future, it could be as simple as email for every firm.

Implementation Considerations:

1. Intended results, audience, and return on investment
    a. Procurement volumes by contractor
    b. Assessment of existing cost of administration
    c. Expected sources of ROI:
        i. Contract leakage
        ii. Partner leakage
        iii. Administration cost
2. Contract rules and complexity
    a. Rebates, volume discounts, price lists
    b. Other high specialized rules or complexity
3. Asset tokenization and payment
    a. Will tokenized assets be exchanged as part of the process
    b. Will payment be done on-chain (Stablecoins) or off-chain
4. Privacy requirements
    a. What does your competition already know about your supply chain (e.g. they probably already know who your major suppliers are)
    b. What's critical to keep a secret (prices, volumes, terms & conditions)

5. ERP integration
    a. How does your ERP output and input purchasing information?
    b. Does your ERP support standardized EDI messages
6. Supplier integration
    a. Will suppliers be able to connect directly to the blockchain?
    b. Will suppliers prefer getting traditional EDI messages?
    c. Will suppliers prefer transacting through a web portal?
7. Supply chain alignment and traceability
    a. Will the assets exchanged be linked to supply chain operations?
    b. How will partners up and down the supply chain gain access to product traceability information? What information will they be allowed to see?

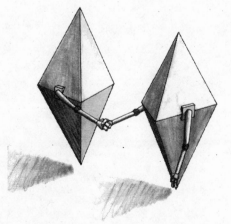

CHAPTER 16

Trade Finance

Most business agreements between companies boil down to "I have money, you have stuff, and we're going to exchange my money for your stuff." Trade finance turns this into a complicated and bureaucratic process involving many different companies, banks, shipping agencies, freight forwarders and more.

Trade finance use cases and letters of credit are not the most common type of global trade. The single most common type of international trade is within enterprises. This usually doesn't require letters of credit as enterprises are able to extend credit internally and arrange payments much more efficiently. Moreover, a lot of international trade is covered by long-standing relationships between relatively large firms that skip the letter of credit process.

Letters of credit and trade finance have an outsize importance to smaller companies, in emerging markets, and where the buyers are the sellers are transacting at arm's length, often around a commodity like raw materials or agricultural outputs. In these cases, there's a need to manage the risks involved for all parties and the extension of credit isn't necessarily automatic.

In these circumstances, the complications that come with trade finance are not arbitrary. Cross-border trade, particularly between far corners of the globe, involves a lot of risk. Things in cross border trade can go very wrong and then either buyers or sellers are left not getting paid for a product that has been delivered or paying for a product that never got made or shipped. Or, even worse, lost somewhere in between.

International trade typically follows a five-step process. First, a buyer and seller reach an agreement on a product sale. Then the buyer's bank provides a letter of credit to the seller guaranteeing payment in exchange for shipment. The seller makes the goods and hands them over to a shipping company, which, in turn, gives the seller a document proving they have accepted the shipment including what it is and where it's going. This is known as the bill of lading.

Once sellers have a bill of lading, they can take it to their bank along with the letter of credit to get paid. The buyer's bank and the seller's bank facilitate the payments. Finally, buyers take their copy of the bill of lading to the shipping carrier to receive the goods being shipped to them. Payment terms are set in the main transaction agreement. These are known as "Inco" terms and some very common ones include "Free On Board" (FOB), which means that payment is due when the product is on the ship, or "Delivered, Duty Paid" (DDP), meaning the product has been delivered to the customer's door and all taxes and duties have been paid.

Into this relatively simple mix, there are typically a few complications that can arise on the path to digitization. The first is that, in addition to the buyer and seller and their banks and the shipping companies, there are other parties involved. These include inspection services, insurance companies, and government agencies which require taxes and documentation to be provided on imports and exports.

To complicate things further, the regulations on imports and exports are often somewhat flexible. There is a global system of harmonized tariff codes which are supposed to standardize how products are treated and categorized between countries, but in practice they don't actually match very well. Political risk is another factor, as countries can choose to "crack down" on "unfair competition" by raising tariffs or implementing sneaky non-tariff barriers like imposing arbitrary new conditions in the name of "safety" or "environmental protection" at the behest of local competitors.

The World Trade Organization (WTO) is supposed to adjudicate these disputes, but they can take years to resolve. In the meantime, trade can be held up or made significantly more costly.

Business Value Proposition

Trade finance is designed to reduce risks like these for buyers and sellers. Fixing all these complications and reducing risk is not cheap, however. And because so much of international trade requires interactions with government agencies, digitization is often very slow or non-existent. Some governments simply do not permit digital documentation at all.

In addition to the typical financing costs, international trade letters of credit usually add another 0.75% to 1.5% to the cost of goods sold. For high-value trades can be worth several thousand dollars. In emerging markets with higher risks, such as trade in sub-Saharan Africa, these costs can rise to 3-4% of the total product.

The interaction with so many different organizations, many of which do not have up to date technologies, makes trade finance a particularly challenging application for digitization and blockchain technology. But this hasn't stopped companies from trying for many years, albeit with only limited success.

Case Study: TradeLens

Perhaps the most ambitious blockchain-based program in recent years has been TradeLens, a joint venture between IBM and Maersk. TradeLens was an effort to accelerate the digitization of global container shipping and cross border trade, a business that represents about $12 trillion dollars in global commerce.

The idea behind Tradelens was to use a blockchain – in this case Hyperledger – to enable shared digital infrastructure for shipping where all the different parties – buyers, sellers, freight forwarders, shippers, and in some cases governments as well – to maintain shared information instead of maintaining separate data silos.

By eliminating the need to constantly re-enter data or track things manually, significant costs could be taken out of the system for all participants. Additionally, the concept behind TradeLens was intended to include a marketplace for applications and connectivity that would allow third parties to create new applications in this environment.

Though TradeLens signed up a number of companies and ports into their system and enabled integrations to dozens of shipping companies and freight forwarders, the company was shut down due to a lack of clients in 2022, after nearly 5 years in operation.

From the beginning, the fact that TradeLens was a private, permissioned blockchain owned by IBM and Maersk deterred other companies, especially other shipping companies, from joining in. Though the underlying technology was "decentralized", the core business model and operations remained centralized and any other firms that joined would have to do so at a disadvantaged position. Maersk's biggest competitors, CMA CGM and Hapag Lloyd both refused to join.

Case Study: Contour Network

Although the Contour Network is not on Ethereum and doesn't operate on a public blockchain, it is one of the very few trade finance businesses in any blockchain ecosystem that has survived and gained traction with a customer base, and so worth looking at. Contour operates on the R3 Corda Network, which is a private blockchain run largely by a consortium of banks.

The member banks in the Contour network cover 46 countries in the U.S., Europe, Latin America, Asia and Africa and include many of the world's top banks and those with a long history of trade finance. The high concentration of banks with strong trade experience such as Standard Chartered and HSBC has been helpful in getting Contour off the ground, but it is also a major source of complexity for Contour, as everything has to be designed carefully to facilitate global integration without breaking anti-trust rules. The payoff for handing this complexity is that there is no single controlling entity that might deter other industry leaders from joining. This avoids a significant problem that was faced by TradeLens.

Unlike some other efforts in this space, Contour Network has been tightly focused on the Letter of Credit Process. Contour's software uses the R3 network to facilitate the design, editing and exchange of the letter of credit documents between the buyer, seller, and the related banks. While other companies can integrate into this process, much of the offline complexity around things like verifying compliance with trade terms remains in the hands of the banks themselves and all payments are executed through the banking system, not the blockchain.

Contour Network has been growing slowly but consistently since its launch right before the pandemic. Given the pandemic and challenges of running major process and technology sales and change, it's probably too early to tell if Contours steady growth will accelerate for another year or two. Very few private blockchain-based businesses have been successful overall, but it has certainly survived longer than virtually any other company in this space.

Limitations & Design Considerations

Two notable problems make adoption of blockchain-based trade finance a very slow process. The first is centralization.

In this respect, the shut-down of TradeLens is hardly an isolated case. Nearly every blockchain-based international trade solution has shut down in the last few years has been a private blockchain solution. Though built on blockchain technology, these firms were all fundamentally centralized. Sophisticated businesses are reluctant to join such networks lest they find themselves disadvantaged in the long-run. This is doubly true when major incumbents like Maersk are founding entities.

Secondly, nearly all these organizations have taken a "document-centric" approach, focusing on the key documents that are the foundation of international trade such as the letter of credit and the bill of lading. I believe this is a challenge because at the end-of-the-day, I want to buy the product, not the document. Automating the letter of credit process seems like a classic approach that involves taking an offline process and putting it online, without doing any substantial re-engineering.

Future Paths

While there is no case-example yet to prove my point, I believe that tokenization and managing the tokens as the items to be bought and sold is a good path forward for international trade finance. This is the true "blockchain-native" approach. On Ethereum, there are an enormous number of services designed to provide financing and to handle the purchase and sale of tokens.

Tokens work well because they represent structured data about the item that is for sale. If you're exporting memory chips, you can issue one digital token for each memory chip and you can write a smart contract that mimics much of the functionality that exists today in the five-step letter of credit model for trade finance.

Tokens also work better because while the import and export activities are highly regulated and often require extensive paper documentation, the actual sale between the buyer and seller usually does not. This approach means that you can have a purchase and sale agreement online, complete with financing, but still leave freight companies and forwarding agents to handle the physical logistics and paper documentation. This will allow for a more incremental one-step-at-a-time approach to digitizing the work.

There are a number of options for integrating data from carriers and freight forwarders into the blockchain-based trade finance process as well. Primarily, this is through the oracle structure, which allows for external data sources that can do things like verify the existence of an asset or track shipping locations. Oracles can also be used to integrate information from third party inspection services.

One thing that has held back this approach is the lack of privacy. Though some countries like the U.S. publish import/export records as a matter of public record, most companies prefer not to disclose what they are shipping and to whom, as this contains competitive information. With the arrival of blockchain-based privacy solutions starting 2023, I hope we will see a revival in efforts to digitize global trade finance, this time on public Ethereum.

Implementation Considerations

1. Business case / job to be done
   a. What's the main problem being solved with blockchain-based trade finance?
   b. What are the costs of the alternatives?
   c. Where does this fit into the larger picture of supply chain tokenization?
2. Assets to be tokenized
   a. What is going to be sold? How is it going to be represented on-chain?
   b. Are these items fungible or non-fungible?

      c.   Do they contain or are they tagged with QR codes or RFID tags that are easily scanned?

      d.   Are they unique and serialized?

3.   Payment and financing approach and options

      a.   Do you want to complete payment on chain?

      b.   What kind of financing is needed? When should the financing get paid off?

      c.   How much risk is involved? Is this a regular supplier or buyer with low risk of a brand new relationship?

4.   Third party inspection and logistics integrations

      a.   Does your product need or does your process require a third party inspection to verify quality before shipment or before payment?

      b.   If so, can the inspection provided be integrated into the process

5.   Government document requirements / paper document requirements

      a.   Are government documents require or system integrations needed?

      b.   Will a freight forwarder or logistics provider handle that?

      c.   Do documents needed to be scanned and attached to physical shipments or digital tokens?

6.   Privacy requirements

      a.   What information in this process needs to be private?

      b.   What information must be public by law?

      c.   What information is already public or well-known and therefore doesn't need to be concealed (keeping in mind that more privacy requirements always make things more complex in implementation)?

7.   System integrations

      a.   What data sources inside your organization can you tap for most data and avoid manual re-entry?

          i.   Orders

         ii.   Inventory

       iii.   Replenishment

       iv.   Forecasts

         v.   Goods receipts

       vi.   Payment receipts

      b.   What Other system integrations are needed?

BIBLIOGRAPHY

Allison, Ian. "IBM and Maersk Struggle to Sign Partners to Shipping Blockchain," *CoinDesk,* October 26, 2018. https://www.coindesk.com/markets/2018/10/26/ibm-and-maersk-struggle-to-sign-partners-to-shipping-blockchain/.

Anderson, Ole, and Louise Vogdrup-Schmidt. "Rivals Reject Blockchain Solution from Maersk
    and IBM." *Shipping Watch*, May 15, 2018.
    https://shippingwatch.com/carriers/Container/article10602520.ece.
Gooding, Matthew. "IBM-Backed Blockchain Platform We.Trade 'Shutting Down.'" *TechMonitor*,
    July 18, 2022. https://techmonitor.ai/technology/emerging-technology/ibm-backed-
    blockchain-platform-we-trade-shutting-down.
"IMPROVING THE AVAILABILITY OF TRADE FINANCE IN DEVELOPING COUNTRIES:
    AN ASSESSMENT OF REMAINING GAPS." World Trade Organization, April 19, 2014.
    https://docs.wto.org/dol2fe/Pages/FE_Search/FE_S_S009-
    Html.aspx?Id=126864&BoxNumber=3&DocumentPartNumber=1&Language=E&Window
    =L&PreviewContext=DP&FullTextSearch=.
Jensen, Thomas, Ravi Vatrapu, and Neils Bjorn-Anderson. "Avocados Crossing Borders: The
    Problem of Runaway Objects and the Solution of a Shipping Information Pipeline for
    Improving International Trade." *Information Systems Journal* 28, no. 2 (August 14, 2017).
    https://onlinelibrary.wiley.com/doi/10.1111/isj.12146.
Jovanovic, Marin, Nikola Kostic, Ina Sebastian, and Tomaz Sedej. "Managing a Blockchain-Based
    Platform Ecosystem for Industry-Wide Adoption: The Case of TradeLens." *Technological
    Forecasting & Social Change* 184 (September 2022).
    https://www.sciencedirect.com/science/article/pii/S0040162522005029?via%3Dihub#bb024
    0.
"Komgo: Blockchain Case Study for Commodity Trade Finance." Komgo. Accessed March 5,
    2023. https://consensys.net/blockchain-use-cases/finance/komgo/.
"Komgo Solutions." Komgo. Accessed March 5, 2023. https://www.komgo.io/komgo-solutions/fi-
    solutions.
Sangha, Parm. "Blockchain and Trade Finance." *Techuk.Org* (blog), March 18, 2022.
    https://www.techuk.org/resource/blockchain-and-trade-finance.html.
"Trade Finance Guide for US Exporters." US Departement of Commerce, July 2022.
    https://www.trade.gov/sites/default/files/2021-
    03/Trade%20Finance%20Guide%20Updated%20030421%20FINAL.pdf.
"Trade Finance in West Africa." International Finance Corporation, October 2022.
    https://www.ifc.org/wps/wcm/connect/publications_ext_content/ifc_external_publication_
    site/publications_listing_page/trade-finance-in-west-africa.
Vineyard, Jared. "BlockChain Race: Maersk Gets Second Carrier to Join Its Platform." *Universal
    Cargo*, April 23, 2019. https://www.universalcargo.com/blockchain-race-maersk-gets-
    second-carrier-to-join-its-platform/.
Wass, Sanne. "Trade Finance Industry Remains Hopeful on Blockchain despite Failed Projects."
    S&P Global Market Intelligence, October 27, 2022.
    https://www.spglobal.com/marketintelligence/en/news-insights/latest-news-
    headlines/trade-finance-industry-remains-hopeful-on-blockchain-despite-failed-projects-
    72557910.

Emissions Tracking & Carbon Offsets

The challenges of climate change have the world working towards a net-zero future. Many of the world's leading enterprises have committed to be Net-Zero in their day to day operations by 2030 and some have gone further, committing to total zero including offsetting prior emissions as well.

Regulators are also working globally to start tracking and managing carbon footprints. The starting points are often cap-and-trade rules that require enterprises to manage their total carbon output with the aim that they adopt more efficient processes.

Overall, the industrial world is succeeding generally at driving down total carbon emissions. However, within this overall story of great progress, there remain a lot of significant challenges and gaps. Some of the biggest include:

1. **Migration of carbon-intensive industries.** Governments fear that getting tough on large GHG emitters will cause them to move offshore. The result would be moving the emissions from one country to another, not reducing them.
2. **Falsified emissions and credits** Without global standards and inspection services, it could be relatively easy for companies to conceal their outputs or falsify their offsets.
3. **Double-counted offsets and credits.** Similar to concerns about faked credits, countries also worry that there are few tools for preventing the repeat sale or counting or legitimate credits.
4. **Variable tracking methodologies and definitions.** Wide variations in definitions make it hard to compare outputs or sum total emissions for a particular product across geographic or industry lines.
5. **Siloed national and industry tracking systems.** Since most modern products and services are built on inputs and outputs from multiple industries and often multiple countries as well, siloed national and regional systems will make it hard to consistently track and manage

totals for any one product or service, especially when they cross national boundaries.

Scope 1, 2, and 3 Emissions

There is no global standardized method yet for tracking and managing greenhouse gas emissions or offsets. This is, however, an emerging consensus among enterprises towards the use of an accounting standard known as the Greenhouse Gas Protocol (GHG) protocol. The concept, broadly, is that a consistent approach to definitions and accounting will make it much easier for enterprises and countries to track, manage, and therefore reduce emissions.

In particular, the GHG Protocol is an effort to start addressing issues like double counting of emissions and credits, variable tracking methodologies, and siloes between countries. In addition, the International Standards Organization (ISO) has published a number of official standards documents (the ISO 14064 series) that generally line up with and draw upon the work of the GHG Protocol team.

The key concepts for most business users at a high level from these protocols and standards is that people increasingly recognize three scopes of traceability in GHG emissions. Scope 1 emissions are direct emissions by a company. Scope 2 emissions are indirect emissions from electricity consumption and heating (among other things). Scope 3 emissions are also indirect, and come in two "flavors": upstream emissions and downstream.

Upstream Scope 3 emissions represent all the input emissions including GHGs produced with raw materials, transportation, waste and capital equipment. Downstream emissions represent the usage of sold products, waste or recycling costs and distribution logistics.

The total collection problem across all three scopes can seem daunting and for many companies' downstream control of how people use their products is somewhat limited. Firms can deploy things like software-based energy saving tools, as Microsoft has done with the XBOX video game system. But that is often the exception more than the rule.

My own expectation is that, over time, the GHG tracking will come to resemble Value Added Tax (VAT) models where each firm has a responsibility to track their own carbon emissions (and offsets) as their inputs move through the supply chain. Products and services at the end of the supply chain will represent the cumulative total of all the emissions and offsets that were accumulated along the way. Depending on how the law evolves, companies may need to pay a carbon tax, or a carbon import duty, to fully or partially offset the totals before the product reaches the end consumer.

No countries have implemented such a model yet, though the European Union is considering actions like a Carbon Frontier (effectively an import tax) that would require firms to reduce carbon emissions related to a product imported into the EU.

Although the final shape and implementation of all these carbon rules, taxes, and offset markets are yet to be established at a government level in most of the world, there are some key conclusions that are "sure bets" in preparation for some variation of this model in the future:

1.   Every firm will need to track their emissions and offsets.
2.   They will need to allocate their carbon emissions and offsets across their products and services.
3.   Measurements of carbon emissions and offsets will have to be done in a rigorous and globally accepted manner.
4.   Enterprises will need to document their process and methodology and have it externally audited and verified.

Applying Ethereum to the Problem

Although there are a huge number of challenges in building a global carbon traceability and offset model, there is already a global infrastructure for managing and tracking structured information across company and national boundaries: Ethereum.

In addition to being open and decentralized, Ethereum has some key features that make GHG management a particularly good use case:

1.   **Tokenization control of carbon emissions and offsets.** Not only is tokenization a useful way of quantifying and moving around assets or liabilities, the smart contracts that are used to define tokens can be established to control which entities can mint new tokens and how they can be moved around. As a result, it is possible to set up standardized models of emissions and only allow those organizations which comply with them to mint tokens. Every token for either emissions or offsets can be traced back to an original emitter. This ensures definitions are standardized and that only firms with inspected and verified processes can issue either emissions or offset tokens.
2.   **Product and service tokenization.** Since companies can tokenize their particular products and services on-chain, they can also associate those tokens with their related emissions and offsets.
3.   **Information aggregation and continuity across enterprise boundaries.** This is one of the most powerful and useful features of

Ethereum. Unlike nearly all enterprise systems, data is not re-entered each time an asset moves from one firm or location to another. Instead, token ownership moves from one wallet to another and data is appended to the token history. Companies can then produce a provable history of the token without gaps.

4. **Oracles for the integration of external data.** Oracles permit the integration of external data into the blockchain. This can be anything from emissions data to location information for products, allowing them to be tracked around the world.

5. **Process and data verifiability to prevent double counting/spend.** Ethereum automatically reconciles all transfers from origin to destination. Blockchains do the kind of transfer reconciliation that banks do for money. The result is really useful in preventing tokens that, say, represent a limited offset capacity of a particular carbon sink or service, from being duplicated and resold.

6. **Data Permanence.** Carbon output reporting by suppliers, when written to the blockchain, will be stored forever, even after the supplying company has come and gone.

Universal distributed ledgers for carbon emissions and offsets will enable firms to show, and prove, that their emissions and their offsets sum to zero. And they will be able to show how they got there and all the sources involved.

As advanced as the concepts may be for managing and tracking carbon and achieving net-zero, the actual use cases that are verifiably deployed today are very limited. The lack of industrialized privacy technology has meant that nearly every tracking effort has been executed on a private blockchain. Additionally, until there are clear deadlines and legislation, there is some lack of urgency around implementing optional rigor in accounting.

Case Study: Setting Standards for Carbon Tokenization

One of the biggest obstacles to getting global emissions properly tokenized, track, and then offset is agreeing upon standards for that tokenization process. Understandably, regulators are wary of the risks of greenwashing or setting standards that are too easy to game.

The Global Blockchain Business Council, in cooperation with the Interwork Alliance, has been developing a standard for tokenization. As a part of this, there are four key pieces of work that are required:

First, a taxonomy is needed so we can understand, characterize, and classify different aspects of carbon reporting. The taxonomy also helps us establish a common language, common terminology, that can be easily understood by all interested parties, from businesspeople to technical implementors.

From the taxonomy, a data model needs to be established that makes it easy to understand the emissions activity. This includes understanding the generating object, what are you doing to generate emissions, the entity doing that work, and where it fits in the widely accepted scope boundaries.

Thirdly, we must define the "behaviors" associated with those tokens. Can they be transferred, and, if so, by whom and under what circumstances? How can we assure that entities cannot "unload" responsibility for their emissions but at the same time make emissions (and the related offset activities) transactable to encourage a global market and investment in carbon reduction and offsets.

This area has perhaps the most ambiguity at the moment. The Scope 1, 2, 3 emissions model doesn't necessarily make tracking and attributing emissions as they go along the supply chain easy to track, particularly the definition of Scope 3 emissions. One alternative path is the possibility of using an approach similar to VAT tracking, where emissions and offsets are passed with finished goods along the supply chain so, at any given point, the total value added and the total emissions in the process are measurable.

Finally, as with anything that gets tokenized, you need to select a token standard. The most common standards are ERC-20 and 721, the fungible and non-fungible standards. The GBBC-IWA working group is closing in on ERC-3525, a proposed standard that is designed to blend a bit of both fungible and non-fungible components. With the semi-fungible token standard, carbon output can be treated as fungible, but you can add metadata to each output showing history and source information.

In the end, the ideal output is one where widely accepted global standards emerge for both carbon output and offsets. Net zero ecosystems will be produced by incentivizing companies to drive down total carbon consumption and to offset that which is absolutely necessary. The math should, in theory, be simple: Carbon Emissions − Carbon Offsets = 0.

Future Path

The combination of specific legislation or taxes as well as a carbon frontier implemented by the European Union could turn all of these baby steps into a stampede for real implementation. The requirements by many governments, such as those in California, that firms disclose their consumption and tracking methodologies are already starting to accelerate the market. In the meantime, standards bodies and leading firms are continuing to work on definitions and concepts that can be implemented.

Implementation Considerations

1. Measurements
   a. Even before tokenization, how will your company measure carbon inputs and outputs?
   b. What are the systems that generate carbon?
   c. How are the carbon outputs measured?
   d. What certifications or tests are required to validate these measurements?
2. Tokenization
   a. Which token standard will be used to track outputs?
3. External Verification
   a. What external audit or verification organizations does your industry require?
4. Inputs
   a. What are the sources of carbon in your business operation?
   b. How are those added to your own usage?
5. Outputs
   a. When products or services leave your organization, what is the total carbon on per-product basis?
6. Scope Alignment
   a. How do each of your inputs and outputs align to the Scope 1,2,3 model?
   b. How much control or influence do you have over Scope 3 emissions from your product?
7. Privacy
   a. Since emissions are often a good proxy for output or inputs and therefore the state of your business, what kinds of privacy controls are needed on granular emissions data?
   b. How will you aggregate emissions data and use private, but on-chain data to prove zero or low emissions without disclosing sensitive business information in real time?

BIBLIOGRAPHY

Bharadwaj, Manu. "Carbon Traceability on the Blockchain." *TraceX* (blog), March 9, 2022. https://tracextech.com/carbon-traceability-on-the-blockchain/.

European Commission. "Blockchain for Climate Action." Accessed March 5, 2023. https://digital-strategy.ec.europa.eu/en/policies/blockchain-climate-action.

Boehmer, Kevin, and Chan Kook Weng. "Launching of ISO 14064 for Greenhouse Gas Accounting and Verification." International Standards Organization. Accessed March 5, 2023. https://www.iso.org/files/live/sites/isoorg/files/archive/pdf/en/greenhouse.pdf.

Climate Trade. "Cabify Leads the Offset of CO2 Emissions with Blockchain." Accessed March 5, 2023. https://climatetrade.com/portfolio-items/cabify-leads-the-offset-of-co2-emissions-with-blockchain/.

"ISO 14064, International Standard for GHG Emissions Inventories and Verification." United States Environmental Protection Agency. Accessed March 5, 2023. https://www3.epa.gov/ttnchie1/conference/ei16/session13/wintergreen.pdf.

"ISO 14064-1:2018 Greenhouse Gases — Part 1: Specification with Guidance at the Organization Level for Quantification and Reporting of Greenhouse Gas Emissions and Removals." International Standards Organization, December 2018. https://www.iso.org/standard/66453.html.

"ISO 14064-1:2018(En) Greenhouse Gases — Part 1: Specification with Guidance at the Organization Level for Quantification and Reporting of Greenhouse Gas Emissions and Removals." International Standards Organization. Accessed March 5, 2023. https://www.iso.org/obp/ui/#iso:std:iso:14064:-1:ed-2:v1:en.

"ISO 14064-2:2019 Greenhouse Gases — Part 2: Specification with Guidance at the Project Level for Quantification, Monitoring and Reporting of Greenhouse Gas Emission Reductions or Removal Enhancements." International Standards Organization, April 2019. https://www.iso.org/standard/66454.html.

"Scope 1 and Scope 2 Inventory Guidance." United States Environmental Protection Agency, September 9, 2022. https://www.epa.gov/climateleadership/scope-1-and-scope-2-inventory-guidance.

Sotos, Mary. "Scope 2 Guidance." *GHG Protocol* (blog), 2015. https://ghgprotocol.org/scope_2_guidance.

"Sources of Greenhouse Gas Emissions." United States Environmental Protection Agency, August 5, 2022. https://www.epa.gov/ghgemissions/sources-greenhouse-gas-emissions.

Kalima.io. "Things You Need to Know about Carbon Tracking Blockchain," October 20, 2022. https://www.kalima.io/post/things-you-need-to-know-about-carbon-tracking-blockchain.

CHAPTER 18

Government and Public Sector Applications

The idea of transparency in government is not new. Louis Brandeis, an American lawyer, famously coined the phrase "sunlight is the best disinfectant." The ability for people to understand what and how their government is operating and how it is spending their money is one of the basic tenets of good governance. It's no accident that the world's leading public-sector anti-corruption group is called Transparency International.

Public blockchains, especially Ethereum, look like an ideal vehicle for executing public sector transparency at scale. Transactions on Ethereum are immutable and public and so is the business logic behind them. From the earliest days of blockchain technology, public accountability advocates have argued in favor of deploying blockchain technology across the public sector.

In reality, progress has been relatively slow. Just like enterprise users, public sector entities are not always comfortable with complete and total transparency. Voters may like absolute transparency, but public sector staff are not necessarily in favor of the endless micromanagement and second guessing that might accompany such extreme transparency. Just like enterprise users, public sector staff are also wary of the complexity of integrating new technologies unless there is a compelling business case.

Myriad Value Propositions

Moving elements of public sector services onto the Ethereum blockchain offers a large range of benefits. Most of them have direct analogues in the commercial world, so I won't cover them in this chapter. Governments, just like corporations, buy stuff, arrange volume discounts and track assets and pay for people's time, services, and products.

There are three notable aspects of public sector work that look very different from private sector requirements. The most obvious is that public sector work is intended to benefit the public, not necessarily maximize profits. This means that equity, fairness, and larger-scale public-good considerations can take precedence over lowest costs or fastest times to deliver.

The second one is the sheer scale of public sector investment. National budgets are far larger than virtually any comparable private sector budget. That means that transaction volumes and value would instantly make government entities the largest or among the largest players in the space.

Finally, governments themselves have special coordination challenges because they do not answer (except in the most voluntary of ways) to other governments. This means that private blockchains, for example are not likely to ever really be acceptable as systems for international collaboration between rival countries. Only a fully public and decentralized system could be a neutral ground between countries for digital transactions.

There are many value propositions that apply specifically or especially well to the public sector. I see five in the near future that are either here now or moving in the right direction to become reality:

1. Verifiable Documentation: A simple process that allows public agencies to go on record about rules and outputs and time-stamp and verify documents using the public Ethereum network.
2. Chain of Custody / Evidence: Similar to other types of asset and product traceability, evidence custody and history is immensely important in court cases. Public Ethereum provides a tamper-proof method for tracking history.
3. Asset Management: The public sector is the biggest investor and owner of assets on the planet. Tracking, managing, and getting the most out of those assets could be immensely valuable as a public service.
4. Spend Accountability: This is one of the biggest opportunities. Corruption and poor spending often cause a loss of confidence and so transparency could help restore public confidence in how taxes and grants are spent.
5. National Security Supply Chains: Advanced technologies often move between countries, but when they are part of a defense supply chain, tracking their movements and custody becomes a matter of national security. Ethereum can be a secure, tamper-proof mechanism for enabling full traceability.

While all these use cases might be valuable, I've selected the focus on spend accountability as the most specific to the public ecosystem for three case studies. The others all have close analogs in the private sector and the last one, defense and security, still remains largely theoretical rather than practical.

Case Example: Gitcoin UNICEF Grants

In 2022, Gitcoin, a public-service oriented Decentralized Autonomous Organization (DAO) organized a series of public goods grants in cooperation with UNICEF, the United Nations International Children's Emergency Fund. The idea behind the Gitcoin's public goods funding model is that uses a blend of total funding and grass roots support to identify projects that have both the support of major donors and those of recipients and individuals who are critical to making these projects successful.

Gitcoin grants are executed on the public Ethereum blockchain with full transparency, and donors agree to be bound by the rules of the quadratic funding process (see the chapter on DAOs and the discussion of how that works in more detail.). In the 2022 pilot, 10 initiatives were selected for funding including programs on financial inclusion, public health, and education.

The concept is that high levels of transparency and the blended approach to funding and selecting grantees will increase the likelihood of program success.

Case Example: Managing Global Contributions with IFAD

IFAD, the International Fund for Agricultural Development, has a wide-ranging global mission to support farmers and families in emerging markets where agriculture remains one of the biggest industries. One of the biggest challenges that multi-national agencies like IFAD face is the need to show donor countries how their funds are being used and generating results.

To help manage this complexity, they are testing out the use of EY's Public Finance Manager, an Ethereum-based blockchain solution for tracking funds and aligning outputs. One of the first pilot projects, an agricultural lending and funding program in Kenya is an excellent illustration of how challenging this in any environment.

Agricultural support funding is critical to support development in countries like Kenya, where farming represents nearly 33% of GDP, compared to between 4-6% in many mature markets. Farmers have less access to capital and need more support in everything from family nutrition to loans to insurance. IFAD works through national governments to try to implement this support.

Funding comes from many different countries supporting the UN and goes through the Kenyan Ministry of Agriculture, Livestock, and Fisheries (MoALF) and from there on to farmers, banks, cooperatives, and retailers to support the sale of insurance, fertilizer, farm equipment and access to credit. The goal is to improve farm output and improve food security for farming families.

Proving cause and effect is extremely challenging because money flows through so many different steps down to individual farmers and nearly every step in that process has disconnected IT systems. Kenya is fortunate to have strong national wireless networks and Africa's best mobile payments system, with MPesa, which makes it possible to have digital traceability from donor country through IFAD, onto MoALF, to companies and cooperatives, and down to individuals. The blockchain-based Public Finance Manager solution is designed to integrate that data and connect it across the network back to donors in a verifiable manner.

If the initial pilot is successful, the program will be expanded and used to increase overall donor support and weed out less efficient aid programs.

Case Example: Fighting Corruption with the International Monetary Fund

Another example of how Ethereum can have a positive impact on the public sector is the International Monetary Fund's (IMF) implementation of Public Finance Manager to track funding and fight corruption. The perception of corruption is one of the key obstacles to increased foreign aid funding in many countries, and so successful efforts to combat corruption not only increase the amount of aid being offered but also improve the value that aid is contribution to recipient countries.

In this case, the IMF and the Ministry of Finance in Guinea Bissau are running a joint project to reduce payroll fraud inside the government. Money from the IMF goes through the Guinea Bissau ministry of finance and gets disbursed to other government agencies to support staffing and programs. The Public Finance Manager system on Ethereum is used to link individual payroll identifiers (with identities protected) to funding commitments and match those with actual employees doing the work. Fantom payroll IDs won't be matchable in this system and the ministry of finance will be able to cut off payments and save money.

The system is in a pilot stage funded by the IMF and could be deployed with other countries as well in the effort to achieve similar anti-corruption goals.

Solution Design Considerations and Limitations

The single biggest solution limitation that I have observed in this space is the lack of privacy. To those new to public sector procurement and anti-corruption work, this seems jarring and incongruous. I imagined when I started on this journey with some of my colleagues that even if we could not get the private sector to use supply chain and spending tools without privacy, we could get the public sector to do so.

In fact, we found that was not the case. Time and again, public sector leaders told us, discreetly, that a system that exposed every aspect of the government spending and procurement process to full public view would not be accepted or adopted. This means that even systems that are designed to support anti-corruption tools are running with privacy controls of private forks of Ethereum.

This is disappointing, because I am still a big believer in the power of public visibility to improve performance and accountability. But I can see some of the value of the critique. An extreme focus on total visibility could make it easy for people to "game the system" by submitting lowest cost bids with no real capacity to deliver or trying to game the system. Civil servants need some discretion to interact with partners and to give them opportunities to improve performance.

I believe the maturing of privacy technologies will allow for a model of selective transparency that preserves the roles of discretion and judgment but still allows for verification of overall performance and comparison of results in a public and verifiable manner. In this way, we can move the process away from private blockchains and on to public Ethereum, which is by far the most accessible and scalable blockchain.

Implementation Considerations

1. What is your specific use case and value proposition?
   a. Notarization
   b. Grand management
   c. Procurement / Spend Accountability
   d. Asset management
   e. National Security
2. What's different about the public sector use case?
   a. Full transparency
   b. Partial transparency
   c. Non-financial goals
3. Who are the stakeholders?
   a. Civil servants
   b. Voters / Members of the public
   c. Multi-national institutions
   d. National/regional governments
   e. Corporations and NGOs

4. What are the key success metrics?
    a. Usage
    b. Outcomes (financial, nonfinancial)
5. How will funding / usage decisions be made?
    a. Donor driven
    b. Political
    c. User-driven
    d. Blended models
6. What systems integrations are needed to track funds and results?
    a. National governments
    b. Payment systems
    c. Non-financial systems / subjective reporting
    d. Banking systems
    e. Other systems
7. What kinds of privacy and transparency are needed?
    a. Can it all be done in full public view
    b. Should there be snapshots / selected visibility
        i.   Initial funding
        ii. Vendor / partner selections
        iii. Outcomes
        iv. Other interim snapshots
    c. What kinds of "Freedom Of Information" or other tools do stake-holders have to verify performance or hold people accountable without violating privacy or constraining good judgment?

BIBLIOGRAPHY

Gitcoin Blog. "Gitcoin <> UNICEF: A Powerful Quadratic Funding Collaboration Pilot." Accessed March 16, 2023. https://go.gitcoin.co/blog/gitcoin-unicef-qf-collaboration-pilot.

CHAPTER 19

Payments and Asset Transfers

"Bitcoin: A Peer-to-Peer Electronic Cash System" is the original title of the 2008 Bitcoin Whitepaper and it says it all: the origin of the world's most widely used cryptocurrency is around the payments use case. I think it's no accident that Bitcoin is not called a digital payment system; it's called electronic cash. Its cash can be transferred on a peer-to-peer basis without any operational complexity or third-party intermediaries.

The foundations for demand for cryptocurrencies were laid back in the 1970s and 1980s with two important developments: digitization of the banking and payment system, and the expansion of KYC and AML laws.

Digital banking didn't just speed up financial services, it also made them much more useful for many people. Holding large amounts of cash is risky and the cost of international payments and remittances is high, especially for individual users. Digital banking offered simpler, faster, and cheaper options, but many people could not access the banking system due to a lack of sufficient documentation required to open an account.

At the same time as banking was getting more useful, it was also becoming less accessible. KYC and AML laws in the US had their origins in the 1970s, but it wasn't until the 1990s and then later in 2001 under the Patriot Act that governments obtained significant powers to review and restrict access to banking services. The bar for getting and opening and account was getting higher. Additionally, a lack of competition meant that although digitization was driving down cost over time, those benefits were not getting passed along to most users, especially in emerging markets.

The growing restrictions on access to digital payments and banking in the U.S. and Europe had a large impact on countries where high inflation and weak government had led to informal dollarization. In those countries there was demand for digital payments and currency, especially U.S. dollars, but governments typically fought hard against dollarization because it undermined their own financial sovereignty.

Bitcoin created a globally accessible and fully decentralized payments system that was theoretically accessible to anyone, operated like cash. The core ideas behind Bitcoin were not just to operate like a digital form of cash, but to improve upon some key shortcomings of cash-based systems all around the world. Most importantly: the danger of central authorities abusing their power and debasing the currency by printing too much of it, resulting in high inflation.

While there's quite a bit of academic debate about whether or not a little bit of inflation is bad, such as rates between 2-5% annually, there's no debate about how damaging inflation can be in countries where it runs out of control, hitting 30%, 40% or 100% or more each year. The result is devastating for the population, especially lower income people who do not have access to inflation-resistant assets like real-estate or business investments.

I would argue that demand for cryptocurrencies is really a proxy for demand for digital payment systems that are widely accessible and based on stable currencies, and that if such things were available everywhere there would be no demand for Bitcoin.

Bitcoin Can't Live Up to Its Hype

Bitcoin itself was designed purely for payments. It doesn't support smart contracts and only marginally supports the definition of other types of assets. First and foremost, it is a currency and a payment system.

Unfortunately, even though Bitcoin is a brilliant technological design and it solved some critical problems that people had not worked through previously, it turns out to be a terrible currency and a terrible payment system, both for individuals and enterprises. Some of the key challenges in Bitcoin include:

- **Proof of Work**. This was a brilliant system at the time it was invented. It prevents collusion between parties and assures a high level of decentralization. Unfortunately, it doesn't scale up very well, leading to very high expenditure to process transactions. This problem has been partially solved with improvements like the Lightning Network, a solution for high volume transaction processing, although this system has not gained much traction as yet.

- **Limited currency minting**. While the concept is clever – taking away the ability of politics to influence central banks – it turns out that algorithms are not mature enough to maintain price stability. The deflationary-by-design model of Bitcoin in particular would be an economic catastrophe if widely adopted. It's also based on some incorrect assumptions among many that central banks in the U.S. and Europe are driven by politics. They are not. The design of independent central banks, with their appointment of multiple governors and overlapping terms seems to work very effectively. While inflation does go up and down slightly in the developed world, no country with an independent central bank has suffered runaway hyperinflation.

- **Cryptocurrency.** Very simply, for people and enterprises who use a national currency for their income and debts, holding significant assets in a different currency is risky and not recommended.
- **Lack of Privacy.** Bitcoin has no privacy by design, and while extreme transparency appeals to some, it has little appeal to many others who consider privacy a foundational human right.
- **Lack of Regulatory Compliance.** Even as KYC and AML systems have come under immense criticism for their cost, complexity, and frequent failure to work, the idea that we should give up on regulatory compliance entirely, and allow bad actors to launder and transfer money without restriction, is a point of view not widely shared.

Tokenization on Ethereum Works Better (Sometimes)

While Bitcoin is not effective either as a currency or a digital asset, Ethereum offers the ability for anyone to define any kind of asset. This opened a path to defining stablecoins and enabling them for payment. Programmable stablecoins offer to enterprise and individual users what Bitcoin lacks: a fiat-currency denominated offering that can be used without embracing foreign-currency risk. (Assuming that a stablecoin is available in your firm's preferred currency.)

You can read more about stablecoins and CBDCs in other chapters in this book. But, for this chapter, I want to focus on the payments use case and in particular, to explain why even for payments, individuals and enterprises should use Ethereum thoughtfully in those cases where it genuinely adds value and not reflexively simply because it is possible. Payments are the best single example I can think of where the actual value of blockchains is specific and limited.

The core issue with payments for enterprise users is not cost. Blockchains are not particularly efficient payment systems, though there are sometimes special circumstances with cross-border or peer-to-peer payments that make it economic. This is perfectly logical if you think about it critically: the Ethereum network has more than 10,000 nodes. Every node gets a copy of every transaction. I don't know how many servers are in the networks of Visa, AmEx, and Mastercard, but I very much doubt that transactions are tested and duplicated to anything like the same degree.

This means that fundamentally, the cost of processing a centralized transaction is far lower than the cost of processing a decentralized one. Debit card transactions typically cost as little as $0.25. Checks cost an average of around $1.50 to process and mobile money systems like M-Pesa charge rates at or below 1% of transaction value.

Blockchain transaction processing is, on average, more expensive. The average bitcoin transaction fee in recent years has been around $1.40, and the average for Ethereum has been around $0.65. However, neither Ethereum or Bitcoin can presently handle the billions of daily transactions processed on other systems.

There are two areas where Ethereum is likely to have a significant advantage over any other payment system. First, where those payments are an integrated part of a larger transaction process based on a smart contract. All traditional payments systems operate in a manner that is disconnected from the rest of the transactional activity. This works nicely for simple payments like buying food in a store.

For more complex payments, where the money represents the completion or an integrated part of a more complex process, Ethereum turns out to have a much better value proposition because execution of the actual payment turns out to be a very small part of the total cost of executing the overall transaction or service. For most enterprises, it can cost up to $100 to approve payment on an invoice when the cost of labor and verification is included. On Ethereum, if all the other components of the agreement are tokenized or part of a smart contract, the cost for completing the transaction is the same as the cost of payment. Now the total cost for the transaction has decreased by as much as 99%.

The second case example where Ethereum is superior to the alternatives is when it comes to transferring assets. Tokenization on Ethereum means that transactions for any asset transfer are all basically the same (token). Moving digital tokens that represent real estate, stocks, bonds, or cars all costs the same on Ethereum as a payment, and in all of these cases, that's far less than the cost of doing so on stock exchanges and land registries.

Two areas are cross border payments and payrolls. Both are tempting but should be treated with caution, because they are subject to a lot of complex regulations. Cross-border payments using crypto can be fast and much cheaper than traditional payment models, but if they bypass a nation's currency controls or regulatory compliance, using them could store up trouble. It's especially tempting for countries where dual exchange rates and currency controls are specifically designed to put multinationals at a disadvantage and getting around them legally is hard.

Paying employees in cryptocurrencies has, at times, been popular as well, but high currency volatility creates risks. Since nearly all employee costs are based in a national currency, including food, rent, and taxes, paying staff in crypto can result in dizzying variations in their pay month to month. It's very popular when crypto is going up but can be catastrophic during a crypto-crash when an employee's pay might drop by 75% in a few months or they lose their entire life savings to a hack or a fraudulent exchange.

Despite these challenges and risks, there are an increasing number of maturing enterprise payment and asset custody and transfer solutions available and more and more firms are adopting these capabilities. And there is a growing ecosystem of related consulting and security services attached to these core capabilities as well.

Case Study: Circle Payments Service

No firm has probably done more to make blockchain-based payments attractive to enterprises than Circle. Their primary product is the network they have built to enable quick payments through blockchains and the banking system primarily covering fiat currencies like the U.S. dollar and the Euro, but also supporting the biggest crypto-native assets – Bitcoin, Matic, and Eth.

Circle has built a set of APIs (Application Program Interfaces) that allow companies to easily manage their accounts in a way that looks similar to brokerage, or bank accounts to enterprise systems and, on top of that, offers solutions for cross-border payments and treasury services, all built on their security and custody systems. The firm's custody solutions also support other types of digital assets and NFTs.

Circle is investing in audits, security systems, identity tools and AML (Anti-Money Laundering) tools on the assumption that most of the existing rules applied in finance today, will be applied equally to crypto and digital assets.

Key Conclusions for Enterprise Users

Payments, particularly in cryptocurrency, in and of themselves are not compelling enterprise use cases. Asset transfers and payments as part of a smart contract do represent significant value creation opportunities. Enterprises will need to proceed with caution to make sure they are not violating securities or money laundering regulations when doing so, however.

When enterprises choose to use blockchains for asset transfers and payments, they will need to carefully consider the custody and control solutions they chose as these will have to be as well designed and implemented as their current, very mature, banking interfaces.

At the conclusion of this chapter, the complexity of custody and payment solutions can look daunting. Doing payments right is difficult and, while banks have had more than a century to build and adapt regulation, the crypto ecosystem is relatively immature. Things that happen behind the scenes in banking look messy and complicated in crypto. (Trust me, they're messy and complicated in banking too, just much more invisible.)

The most common enterprise strategy is to actually start with the non-financial components of the process and gradually move towards both integrating payments and treating digital asset tokens as digital assets. What this means in practice is that early on, if a firm wanted to use a smart contract for procurement, it might choose to create digital tokens to represent products being bought or sold. However, those tokens might exist only for tracking purposes, not redeemable for the actual assets and payments would be executed off-chain. (I don't see this as an ideal end-state, bur rather as a messy but safe interim step as firms get comfortable.)

In this early-stage environment, disaster then isn't very disastrous. If someone hacks into your system and steals your asset tokens, well, they've stolen the product tracker, not the actual product. That's a data corruption problem you have to fix, not a major theft you need to report to the board of directors.

Over time, firms will evolve their approach, imparting value to the asset tracking tokens and eventually choosing to complete payments on-chain. By then, they should have confidence that their digital asset competency and partners are as strong as their traditional banking partners and processes.

Implementation Considerations

1. What is the problem to be solved with a blockchain-based payment or asset transfer system?
    a. Is this for cost reduction?
    b. Are you evading national regulatory or currency controls?
    c. Do you really want to hold significant value in highly volatile crypto assets?
2. What assets are to be used in the payments and transfers?
    a. Are you going to use crypto assets like Eth and BTC?
    b. Do you plan to tokenize, hold and transfer other types of assets
3. What are the major regulatory compliance requirements?
    a. How will you assure KYC and AML and customer identity
    b. Is the stablecoin itself regulated? By which entity?
4. What kinds of custody, security and implementation tools are needed?

    a.   How will you secure these assets?

    b.   What custody system will be used

5.   What enterprise systems integration will be required?

    a.   How will you integrate this to your production or payment systems

6.   What kind of enterprise business controls are needed?

    a.   What kinds of controls do you need to implement? Are those controls equal or comparable to controls being implementing with other banking and payment partners?

    b.   Will you need to obtain a Systems of Control (SOC) report from an auditor?

7.   What is the end -state goal and long-term path for getting there?

    a.   What is your end state goal? Are these payments set to happen on a stand-alone basis or are they part of a smart contract

    b.   How does your firm plan to come up the risk/experience curve without creating significant exposure

    c.   What business partners who have more experience are being drafted in to help this process?

SOURCES:

"Average Ethereum Transaction Fees." Ethereum average transaction fee. Yahoo, January 26, 2023. https://ycharts.com/indicators/ethereum_average_transaction_fee

Comply Advantage. "Anti Money Laundering History: 1970 to 2022," 2023 226AD. https://complyadvantage.com/insights/us-anti-money-laundering-act-amla-history/.

"Average Bitcoin Transaction Fees." Yahoo Finance, January 26, 2023. https://ycharts.com/indicators/bitcoin_average_transaction_fee.

"MPesa Transaction Fees," January 26, 2023. https://www.monisnap.com/gb/blog/post/m-pesa-sending-charges/.

"Here Are the Updated M-PESA Transaction Charges for 2023," January 17, 2023. https://www.dignited.com/74281/m-pesa-charges-2023/.

Vodacom Tanzania. "M-Pesa Transaction Fees - (Effective from 03rd September 2021)," n.d. M-Pesa Transaction fees - (Effective from 03rd September 2021).

PayJunction. "The True Cost of Paper Checks." Accessed January 26, 2023. https://blog.payjunction.com/paper-checks-ach.

"Debit Card Processing Fees." Accessed January 10, 2023. https://www.lendio.com/blog/debit-card-processing-fees/.

Nakamoto, Satoshi. "Bitcoin: A Peer-to-Peer Electronic Cash System." Accessed January 23, 2023. https://bitcoin.org/bitcoin.pdf.

CHAPTER 20

Central Bank Digital Currencies

Despite whitepaper titles like "Digitizing Money," most money is, in fact, already digital. In the United States, 97% of all money today is already digital so when people talk about "digitizing" the national currency, what they are most often talking about these days is the creation of a Central Bank Digital Currency (CBDC).

CBDCs are not intended to be like other forms of digital money. Nearly all digital money today is created in the banking system and is controlled and managed by private entities in bank accounts, credit cards and other payment and deposit systems. The Federal Reserve (standing in here as a typical central bank) acts as a lender of last resort and national clearinghouse, but it cannot see detailed transactional information on all or indeed most of the money that's in circulation.

CBDCs are intended to operate more like physical cash – which is all minted and controlled by the Federal Government. Instead of physical bills, digital cash can be moved from one wallet to another, but the Federal Reserve would maintain visibility and, potentially, some form of control, over all that cash.

Although China can rightly be credited with kicking off the interest in digital currencies, it is most likely that the current explosion of projects can be traced to the rise of bitcoin and blockchain-based stablecoins, like Circle's USDC. Central bankers started to worry about two potential problems: the first was that digital currencies like bitcoin offered some value proposition that was more attractive than a national currency. Bitcoin-maximalists often claim that bitcoin is superior to national fiat currencies because it empowers the unbanked and because it insulates people from the bad decisions of politically motivated central bankers.

The second fear central bankers had was that even if the national currency was more attractive than bitcoin or some other global crypto-asset, if that success came in the form of a fiat-currency denominated digital coin (often referred to as a stablecoin), it would be beyond the reach of traditional central bank regulation and they would, effectively, lose control of the money supply. That might further extend to a loss of control and visibility to the economy as a whole and the government's ability to collect taxes. Products like MakerDAO, which are algorithmic stablecoins that have no dollars in them, were particularly of concern, as they allow for transactions in "dollars" without any actual dollars.

Creating a tokenized, blockchain-based national digital currency offers banks at least one option in preparing a competing alternative to cryptocurrencies and digital stablecoins.

CBDC Solution Approaches

At the time of this writing, there are more than 79 CDBC research programs around the world and eight countries are running pilots, though none have yet deployed at scale. (cbdctracker.org is an excellent source on these developments.) CBDC solution approaches can be bucketed into two categories: wholesale programs and retail programs. Though inspired by blockchain technology and drawing heavily on the example of Ethereum with tokenization, very few of these are actually built on blockchains or any kind, private or public.

Typically, wholesale programs are designed to operate between central banks and member banks. This delegates to member banks the authority to manage business rules and regulatory compliance, such as Know Your Customer (KYC) and Anti-Money-Laundering (AML) rules. Individual banks could then, in turn, issue their own digital currency.

In a sense, these are a bit like a digital version of the model that has existed for some time in Hong Kong, where the Hong Kong Monetary Authority actually delegates the issuance of the local Hong Kong dollar to multiple private banks. The currency is all interchangeable, but consumers get the novelty of bank notes issued by many different banks.

The second approach, and one that is preferred by many central bankers, is a direct-to-retail approach that has the central bank issuing digital tokens to end users. China, India, Nigeria, Ghana, The Bahamas, Jamaica, and Uruguay are all pursuing direct retail CBDC pilot programs, where individual consumers will have a wallet and digital assets directly issued by the government. Though official digital currencies have only been launched as "production" systems in the Bahamas and Jamaica, China's e-Yuan is by far the biggest and most ambitious project so far and the one that much of the world is watching closely.

FOMO and Control – The CBDC Value Proposition

The CBDC value proposition is, to put it bluntly, very weak. Central banks have had a difficult time explaining how they would be useful and what value they add over existing systems that are already widely used, known as Real Time Gross Settlement systems (RTGS). RTGS solutions are in place in more than 90 countries and allow banks, usually through the national central bank, to instantly settle liabilities and payments with each other.

In addition to RTGS systems which serve large banks and corporations and are optimized for settling large payments, many countries also have national payments platforms that are optimized for low-cost, high-speed consumer payments. The U.S., U.K., Singapore, India, Sweden, and Denmark all have national networks for low-cost payments, most of them owned by member banks.

Given that low cost, nearly instantaneous digital payments are available for both enterprises, banks and consumers already exist in many countries, it's not clear if there is a strong value proposition for this new technology in countries that already have RTGS systems. There are some cases, however, where they may be a value proposition:

Competition: In several countries, the market for digital payments is highly consolidated or lacks competition. Implementing a retail CBDC would allow direct consumer-to-merchant digital payments just like cash. China is a particularly good example, where Alipay and WeChat Pay represent something close to 95% of all online payments. This puts immense power in the hands of just two companies. Transaction pricing is low in China, averaging about 0.55%, competitive with most global credit card markets, but AliPay and WeChat Pay dominate and profit extensively from all the related credit and payment services. The U.S. is another example, where credit card interchange fees are 70-80% higher than the global average in a market dominated by just two companies, Visa and Mastercard.

Visibility, compliance and risk management. Both a retail and a wholesale CBDC would provide central banks with more granular visibility as to how money is flowing. Today, central banks have limited visibility to the monetary system. If they run a payments system, they can view loans and settlements moving between banks, but they cannot see how money is flowing within banks nor can they see consumers are spending (or not spending) money or how deposits and redemptions are working. In theory, a centrally-managed CBDC would allow banks to monitor cash transactions all the way down the retail or peer-to-peer level, looking at risk and compliance issues.

Not only is the value proposition weak, but there I see four substantial problems facing CBDC efforts:

Competition. Though CBDCs could be used to increase competition in some areas, like payments, they also represent a form of competition between central banks and commercial banks. A CBDC token issued by a major central bank, say the Federal Reserve or the European Central Bank (ECB), would be more attractive to many people than a bank deposit. Banks can collapse. Central banks cannot. As a result, a Federal Reserved-issued digital dollar carries less risk than any money issued by or held in a commercial bank.

In the normal course of events, this might not be a significant differential. Commercial banks often enjoy a mix of both explicit guarantees (though limited in total value, like Federal Deposit Insurance in the U.S.) and implicit guarantees that governments will not allow them to go bankrupt. In a crisis, the existence of a government issued digital money might accelerate bank runs as deposits switch to the one fully guaranteed asset available.

Programmability. Very simply, none of the CBDCs that have been proposed offer programmability today. You cannot use a government issued CBDC to buy an asset on a public blockchain, like Ethereum, nor can you deposit government issued CBDCs in any decentralized finance service. While both Brazil and China have some degree of programmability on their long-term roadmaps, most central bankers I have spoken to are firmly against implementing programmability because of the long history of DeFi hacks on Ethereum.

Compliance. While regulators and central banks are used to setting Know-Your-Customer (KYC) and Anti-Money Laundering (AML) rules, they have little experience actually applying them. The one form of currency they directly issue to people today is cash, which is subject to neither. It's the main reason people prefer cash for illicit transactions.

As CBDC pilots start to go live, Central Banks are struggling with how to implement KYC and AML rules in software. Some systems, like Nigeria's, require that users already have a bank account with a bank that has a KYC program. This hugely simplifies the sign-up process, but then you have to wonder what the point is of having a digital currency at all, if everyone who has it will also already have a bank account.

Systemic digital risk. One of the great misunderstandings that exists today is that many people outside of the banking and finance sector think that financial services are "centralized." If blockchains are decentralized, then banking must be centralized? No, actually. It isn't. Banking and payments and financial services generally are highly fragmented and, from a technical and operational standpoint, also highly decentralized.

Banks transact with each other through networks with many layers. Regional banks often have regional clearinghouses that handle most payments before larger banks transact with each other on a national or cross-border level. Every bank and central bank has a different system. This introduces many inefficiencies and delays in the system, but it also protects the system from system-wide hacks. Most money may be digital, but "hacking" a national currency is hard because the digital money is spread across so many different forms and digital silos.

Introducing a national digital currency changes all of that: at one stroke, hackers could disable not just some dollars, but all of them. Given the systemic importance of the financial system to the broader economy, such forms of digital integration must be done with great care and deliberation.

Despite the challenges being faced, a mind-boggling number of national digital currency projects are underway. There is hardly a major economy that is not testing or piloting the concept of a wholesale and or a retail CBDC. This book isn't intended as an exhaustive review, but here are two short case examples of CBDCs in pilot stages:

Case Example: Digital Yuan

China's project, known as the e-Yuan or Digital Currency Electronic Payment (DCEP) has been running in various stages since planning started in 2014. Pilot banks were on-boarded in 2017 and a regional pilot started in 2020 and continuing through 2022. Chinese authorities reported that at the end of 2021, 261 million users had wallets but had transacted just $14 billion in payments. That's an average of just $53 per wallet. Much of that money was given away in lotteries with a specific use-it-or-lose-it requirement.

China's CBDC program has been piloted in several cities and many retailers accept payments through QR codes from the CBDC system. Because QR payment codes are already used by Alipay and WeChat pay and cashless payments are already widespread, this has simplified the work required to deploy the system for acceptance. User reports say the user experience is similar to AliPay and WeChat pay.

Case Example: Digital Naira

Nigeria launched the eNaira back in 2021, making it the first CBDC introduced in Africa. The eNaira is based on blockchain technology but it is not a public or open blockchain like Ethereum. The stated goal of the eNaira project is to facilitate financial inclusion, bringing more of the economy into the formal sector, and enable cross-border remittances for Nigeria's large global diaspora.

Nigeria's central bank wants more than 90% of the population to have access to the eNaira.

While the app and service got off to a good start, user reviews suggest the system is struggling. Today, you must already have a bank account in order to use the eNaira, which means it does not really expand the formal sector of the economy of bring in the unbanked. The bank intends to relax that requirement in the future, though accounts without IDs will be subjected to transaction limits. Compared to cryptocurrency adoption, which is estimated to be as high as 50% in Nigeria, adoption of the eNaira has been slow. The Central Bank of Nigeria maintains that use of cryptocurrency is not permitted under the law, but that has had little impact.

In December 2022, the Nigerian government moved to limit cash withdrawals by both individuals and businesses in an effort to speed up the transition to a fully digital payments system. The limits for individuals are approximately $225/week and for businesses $1,200 per week. This appears intended to push users towards cashless options.

The government has not disclosed any plans to enable interoperability with public blockchains or other CBDC systems or enabling of smart contract features.

Bottomline for Enterprises

In the near term, most enterprise users will not be affected by CBDC deployments outside of banking and retail as these likely be pilots for wholesale or retail deployment. Even if CBDCs are eventually widely deployed, it is likely that for most enterprise users, the impact will be little or none as these will be hidden behind existing banking interfaces and will not permit programmability.

One possibility is that in the future, central banks may consider issuing CBDCs on the Ethereum blockchain. Test programs are underway in several countries, but they are at a very early stage. More advanced central banks have started to think through the full set of use cases and challenges they have to deal with the potential value to users. But full implementation by them is several years down the road.

DATA SOURCES:

BNG Payments. "ACH Payment Fees: How Much Does ACH Cost?" Corporate Web Site, August 25, 2021. https://www.bngpayments.net/blog/ach-payment-fees/.

Anthony, Nicholas. "Nigeria Restricts Cash to Push Central Bank Digital Currency." *The Cato Institute* (blog), December 19, 2022. https://www.cato.org/blog/central-bank-digital-currency-war-cash.

Brunnermeier, Markus, and Harold James. "The Digitization of Money." *Bank for International Settlements* (blog), May 19, 2021. https://www.bis.org/publ/work941.htm.

Central Bank of Nigeria. "Naira Redesign Policy - Revised Cash Withdrawal Limits." Central Bank of Nigeria, December 6, 2022. https://www.cbn.gov.ng/Out/2022/CCD/RevisedCashWithdrawal.pdf.

Coinmetrics, and Bitstamp. "The Rise of Stablecoins," 2020. https://f.hubspotusercontent00.net/hubfs/5264302/The%20Rise%20of%20Stablecoins.pdf.

Georgieva, Kristalina. "The Future of Money: Gearing up for Central Bank Digital Currency." *International Monetary Fund* (blog), February 9, 2022. https://www.imf.org/en/News/Articles/2022/02/09/sp020922-the-future-of-money-gearing-up-for-central-bank-digital-currency.

Greene, Robert. "What Will Be the Impact of China's State-Sponsored Digital Currency?" *Carnegia Endowment for International Peace* (blog), July 1, 2021. https://carnegieendowment.org/2021/07/01/what-will-be-impact-of-china-s-state-sponsored-digital-currency-pub-84868.

Clearly Payments. "Interchange Fees by Country." Accessed January 29, 2023. https://www.clearlypayments.com/blog/interchange-fees-by-country/.

Mookerjee, Ajay. "What If Central Banks Issued Digital Currency?" *Harvard Business Review*, October 15, 2021. https://hbr.org/2021/10/what-if-central-banks-issued-digital-currency#:~:text=Over%2097%25%20of%20the%20money,code%20by%20a%20commercial%20bank.

The Business of Business. "Nigeria Touts Its Digital Currency as a Success – Citizens Give It Mixed Reviews so Far," February 18, 2022. https://www.businessofbusiness.com/articles/nigeria-touts-its-digital-currency-as-a-success-citizens-give-it-mixed-reviews-enaira-CBDC/.

Panetta, Fabio. "Central Bank Digital Currencies: Defining the Problems, Designing the Solutions." *European Central Bank* (blog), February 18, 2022. https://www.ecb.europa.eu/press/key/date/2022/html/ecb.sp220218_1~938e881b13.en.html

Ree, Jack. "Five Observations on Nigeria's Central Bank Digital Currency." *International Monetary Fund* (blog), November 16, 2021. https://www.imf.org/en/News/Articles/2021/11/15/na111621-five-observations-on-nigerias-central-bank-digital-currency.

"Regulation II (Debit Card Interchange Fees and Routing)." Board of Governors of the Federal Reserve System, July 25, 2022. https://www.federalreserve.gov/paymentsystems/regii-average-interchange-fee.htm.

Resendiz, Joseph. "The Cost of Accepting Credit Card Payments: NA vs EU." *ValuePengiun* (blog), June 29, 2015. https://www.valuepenguin.com/interchange-fees-na-vs-eu.

Smith, Matt. "Cryptocurrency Usage Soars in Nigeria despite Bank Ban," June 9, 2022. https://www.spglobal.com/marketintelligence/en/news-insights/latest-news-headlines/cryptocurrency-usage-soars-in-nigeria-despite-bank-ban-70497781.

CBDC Tracker. "Today's Central Bank Digital Currencies Status." Reference Data, January 29, 2023. https://cbdctracker.org.

Bank of England. "UK Central Bank Digital Currency," January 12, 2023. https://www.bankofengland.co.uk/digital-currencies.

Ocean Payment. "Wechat Pay / Alipay Fees for Merchants," September 9, 2021. https://www.oceanpayment.com/blog/19775/.

Zimwara, Terence. "Nigerian CBDC Still Not Widely Used a Year After Launch." *Bitcoin.Com News* (blog), October 27, 2022. https://news.bitcoin.com/nigerian-cbdc-still-not-widely-used-a-year-after-launch/.

CHAPTER 21

Stablecoins

CBDCs often seem like a solution in search of a problem. Designed by committee to compete with the popularity of cryptocurrencies and stablecoins, there seems little customer "pull" on these solutions. Stablecoins, by contrast, emerged from nowhere starting in 2014 and have since become the most widely used foundation for transactions on public blockchains other than Bitcoin and Ether themselves.

The appeal of stablecoins is simple: they're stable. The name itself is something of an indictment of cryptocurrencies. While cryptocurrency maxis (as they're known in the industry, especially the Bitcoin maxis), will tell you they are creating a universal digital currency, the reality is that most people don't want cryptocurrency as an actual currency. The volatility of cryptocurrencies makes them unattractive as a currency.

Tether, the first stablecoin, emerged on the Bitcoin blockchain starting in 2014 as a way for traders to "park" their cash between investments without really having to cash out of the blockchain ecosystem. The attraction was that while bitcoin was very volatile, the Tether token would be "tethered" to the value of the U.S. dollar and they would keep the value of assets in U.S. dollars equal to the amount of tokens issued.

The Value Proposition for Stablecoins in the Enterprise

While day-traders and consumers may see stablecoins as valuable for their stability, these digital assets have their own strong value proposition for enterprises: they are available in the currencies in which most firms already do business, especially the U.S. dollar.

The idea that firms would want to do business in cryptocurrency was always a weak one. While crypto may have a value proposition as an investment asset, it doesn't work well for risk-averse enterprises. The idea that a firm, which primarily does business in the U.S. dollar or Euro would want to switch from dollars to crypto, conduct on-chain transactions in crypto, and switch back to dollars doesn't make a lot of sense. Firms would be embracing a great deal of foreign exchange risk and transaction costs.

By transacting in and holding dollar-denominated (or any other major fiat currency) stablecoins, firms reduce risk, eliminate many transaction costs, and can budget and plan in a consistent manner. All things being equal, I expect that most firms will choose to transact in their primary business currencies. Unlike CBDCs, stablecoins like USDC are available on Ethereum and can be integrated into smart contracts, from procurement systems to DeFi.

Three Types of Stablecoins

Three types of stablecoins have emerged over the last few years. The most common type is the fiat-currency denominated, asset-backed stablecoin. These represent the bulk of the market, but they're not the only solutions out there, though it is likely to be the most commonly used by enterprises.

Asset-backed stablecoins: This is by far the most common type. These are usually denominated in fiat currencies like the US dollar and the Euro and they are usually backed by investment-grade commercial and government bonds. There are a number of variations as well such as tokens backed by oil, gold, or other commodities. The best analogy in tra ditional financial markets is a money market fund, which is composed of highly liquid short-term securities, is denominated in a local fiat currency, but pays a slightly higher interest rate than a traditional deposit account.

Most importantly, these assets exist primarily or usually exclusively off-chain and so users must "trust" the firm issuing the tokens to keep sufficient off-chain capital to support redemptions.

Algorithmic stablecoins: These are also asset-backed stablecoins and they are also usually denominated in fiat currencies as well, but typically these are composed entirely of on-chain assets and governed by algorithms that increase or decrease the assets backing each unit of currency as the value of those assets changes. The risk here is that prices swing far enough to break the value of the stablecoin. The benefit, however, is that it is not necessary to trust off-chain asset reserves.

Currency-backed stablecoins: These are similar to asset-backed stablecoins except they solely rely upon national fiat currency in regulated bank accounts. I have heard these referred to as "digital dollars" so as to distinguish them from a more "traditional" stablecoin, though I am not aware of any firms offering these yet. These are specifically designed to be very low risk. The downside is that there is no opportunity for the offering vendor to make money on the deposited assets when interest rates are very low. That means that this type of stablecoin may come with account fees and transaction fees for origination.

In the U.S., these stablecoins may (eventually) also come with an implicit or explicit FDIC guarantee.

Risks and challenges for stablecoin users

Though far less risky than cyrpto-currency, Stablecoins come with their own risks for firms attempting to implement them. There are three major risks that firms should focus on:

Regulatory compliance risk: The regulations governing stablecoins are still very immature. Companies that offer Stablecoins are typically guessing at how existing regulations such as rules governing money market funds might be applied to stablecoins. Some countries, such as Japan, are in the early stages of defining regulations that govern stablecoins. The U.S., U.K. and the EU all have plans to set up emerging digital asset regulatory and stablecoin rules, though at the time of writing these were not yet defined. So far, no enforcement actions have been taken against the most reputable providers, but that has not proven to be very comforting as regulators seem far behind the curve in crypto.

At this time, I'd recommend that firms minimize the amount of transactions they do using on-chain crypto or stablecoins until there's clear regulatory rules. It seems safe for firms to receive payment in crypto as this has been happening for many years, but since KYC and AML rules are not well established or standardized on-chain, this should probably be limited to well known suppliers and business partners.

Verification and Audit Risk: Aside from the risk of unknown regulatory rules, the single biggest risk in the past for Stablecoins has been that those with off-chain reserves are not verified or audited. The largest stablecoin provider, Tether, has admitted that in the past, at times, it failed to maintain the level of reserves needed and it has had several audit firms over the years, none of them from the globally recognized "Big 4."

Some stablecoin providers have been able to have law firms provide attestation to their reserves and others have executed what are known as "Proof of Reserves" audits where users can independently verify that the stablecoin provider has assets equal to on-chain liabilities. The key risk here is that unless the proof of reserves auditor is also the primary financial statement auditor, it may be possible for the stablecoin firm to have liabilities elsewhere that are not visible on chain.

Until the rules are clearly set by regulators, it will be hard to get big audit firms to do the full financial statement audit and agree to also provide continuous proof of reserves attestations. The technology to do so already exists and to provide nearly continuous updates, we're just waiting for the auditors and the regulators to agree upon the process and safeguards.

Software Risk: The final major risk is software risk. Theoretically, you can make software without bugs or security vulnerabilities. In practice, it's safe to assume that most software has some weakness. Two factors that drive up risk are newness and complexity. Simple stablecoin tokens are neither new nor complex, so they represent a low level of risk.

Algorithmic stablecoins are not new either, but they are complex. Enterprises would be advised to steer clear of poorly governed or new algorithmic stablecoins. However, mature algorithmic coins with mature and stable governance processes might be an option, especially for firms or countries where actually having access to the U.S. dollar poses financial or regulatory risks.

Case Examples:

MakerDAO: MakerDAO is the home of Dai, the original multi-collateralized stablecoin. Dai is pegged to the US dollar and is considered the first and by far the most mature multi-collateralized stablecoin, with MakerDAO being founded in 2014 and the first version of Dai launched in 2017. The initial version used only Ether as collateral, but newer versions support multiple types of collateral. In July 2021, there was about $5 billion in Dai circulating on Ethereum backed by approximately $8 billion in collateral.

The MakerDAO foundation and the maker team, led by the original founder, Rune Christensen, have been pioneers in on-chain transparency and governance. Every new form of collateral and every major governance change has been organized and voted upon by the community.

Since 2017, crypto has faced two "crypto winters" and a number of days with enormous swings in asset valuations. The Dai has only "broken" away from the $1 peg a few times and only briefly. There are no other multi-collateralized stablecoins of any size at the moment. Maker's share of the stablecoin market on Ethereum appears to move between about 5-10%.

Stasis euro: Nearly all the stablecoins out there today are U.S.-dollar denominated. In the future, as DeFi becomes more widely deployed, it is reasonable to expect that there will be stablecoins that are linked to each national currency. At the time of writing, there were about $47 million Stasis Euros in circulation and they had been used to settle a little over $5 billion in payments.

The smaller market size today for Euro-based transactions means that the total size and maturity of firms like Stasis is not as well developed, but the firm still has regular audits and is based inside the European Union.

Inside the EU, the Markets in Crypto-Assets (MiCA) legislation, which came into force in April 2023, is designed to lay out the operating framework for cryptocurrency and other digital assets in Europe. However, it has not yet taken effect and it is expected to take effect around January 2024. The MiCA rules cover stablecoins and apply rules similar to banking around issues like capital requirements.

Developed/Not Yet Available: digital dollars. One concern about "traditional" stablecoins is that they are typically backed by liquid financial assets but not necessarily U.S. dollars in regulated bank accounts. The business model of stablecoin issues is to make money primarily on the "float" and, to a lesser extent, on transaction fees. The downside is that, like a money-market fund, is the underlying securities lose significant value, there's a risk that the fund will not have sufficient liquidity to cover all redemptions.

Several firms are contemplating creating something they are calling "Digital Dollars." The idea behind these is that they are an ultra-low-risk form of fiat currency token – backed solely by bank deposits in regulated banks. As such, these would also not be considered securities and not require a securities registration.

The crypto-collapse of 2022 has put most regulatory approvals for new stablecoins and crypto products into slow motion, however, so it could be some time before these products come to market in the U.S.

The Future is Regulated

At this time, there are few if any regulations that are specifically targeted at fiat-currency stablecoins. The British government announced in 2022 that it will specifically bring stablecoins into its payments regulatory framework. Similar discussions are taking place in the U.S. Japan has among the most advanced regulatory frameworks for stablecoins, with locally regulated banks permitted to issue them. Additionally, in December 2022, Japanese regulators announced they will lift the ban on the distribution of international stablecoins within Japan.

Japan's stablecoin rules are a good example of a future regulatory framework. Stablecoins must be issued by banks and backed by cash deposits, so it looks like a model closer to the "Digital Dollar" than a money market fund. The U.S. and U.K. may end up permitting a money-market-fund model as well, though it may have to be registered as a security, since money market funds offered by banks and brokerages are also listed as securities.

Once these payment systems are fully regulated, it will be easier for enterprises to adopt them without any further concerns. In the interim, enterprises may prefer to execute transactions like inventory management on-chain, but settle the financial payment off-chain through the traditional banking system.

Implementation Considerations:

For companies planning to use Stablecoins, not for those planning to build them.

1. What is the primary purpose for using stablecoin?
    a. Enabling payment as part of a smart contract / exchange of goods
    b. Financial investment
    c. Asset management
    d. Cross-border payments
2. What is the expected Value Proposition / ROI?
    a. Reduced transaction cost
    b. Reduced reconciliation complexity
    c. Faster cycle time
3. What are the key risk management considerations?
    a. How much capital will be in this environment, at risk?
    b. Will the company use institutional custody services or manage a wallet?
    c. How will payment controls be enforced? Will it be the same as the banking interface?
4. What is the regulatory climate in the country in question?
    a. Clear regulatory rules
    b. Explicitly permitted
    c. Implicitly permitted (e.g. operators in place and doing business, no recent enforcement actions by regulators)
    d. Explicitly not permitted (then definitely not recommended.)
5. What are the main privacy requirements?
    a. Do the payments need to be private?
    b. What mechanisms will be used to enforce privacy?
    c. What data/metadata is likely to "leak" as part of the payment process? Will that be more or less acceptable compared to other payment options?

DATA SOURCES:

Iwata, Natsumi, and Keita Sekiguchi. "Japan Adopts Law to Regulate Stablecoins for Investor Protection." *Nikkei Asia*, June 3, 2022.
https://asia.nikkei.com/Spotlight/Cryptocurrencies/Japan-adopts-law-to-regulate-stablecoins-for-investor-protection.

Partz, Helen. "Japan to Lift the Ban on Foreign Stablecoins like USDT in 2023: Report." *Cointelegraph*, December 26, 2022. https://cointelegraph.com/news/japan-to-lift-the-ban-on-foreign-stablecoins-like-usdt-in-2023-report.

Schickler, Jack. "UK Stablecoin Rules Approved by Lawmaker Committee." *CoinDesk*, October 27, 2022. https://www.coindesk.com/policy/2022/10/27/uk-stablecoin-rules-approved-by-lawmaker-committee/.

CHAPTER 22

Exchanges

Cryptocurrency exchanges are essential infrastructure in the world of Ethereum. They typically serve three major purposes. The first is to enable people to convert fiat currencies like dollars and euros into crypto-assets like Ethereum or stablecoins. In this capacity, they are acting as on and off-ramps between the traditional banking system and Ethereum.

The second purpose of exchanges is to act as true exchanges inside the world of Ethereum – allowing users to exchange one type of digital token for another. In this capacity, exchanges really act as essential suppliers of liquidity in the ecosystem. Finally, many exchanges offer digital asset custody as well, handling security and storage of digital assets on behalf of their clients.

Two Types of Exchanges

There are two distinct categories of exchanges operating in the world of Ethereum. The most common is what is referred to as a centralized exchange (CEX). Centralized exchanges, like Kraken and Coinbase, are companies with management teams that maintain the links to and from the existing banking system.

Centralized exchanges are essential because without them, the only way to obtain Eth, the foundational currency of Ethereum, would be to mine or earn it yourself, which is impractical for most people. Centralized exchanges are also the place where Know-Your-Customer and Anti-Money-Laundering regulations are most clearly and easily enforced, since you need identification to move assets in and out of the banking system.

Centralized exchanges are also the only kind of exchange that offers custody services. While most centralized exchanges will happily let you purchase a digital asset and then send them to your own wallet for long-term storage. Most users are not sophisticated enough to do that and prefer to keep their assets with the exchange.

The second type of exchange is known as a decentralized exchange (DEX). These exchanges, most prominently Uniswap, do not offer custody. Instead, they only allow people to exchange one type of token for another. As the name implies, these exchanges are indeed fully decentralized. They exist only as software that operates independently on-chain. Users interact with the smart contract directly, exchanging one token for another.

Decentralized exchanges (DEXes) use historical supply and demand data (often provided from external sources) to develop Automated Market Makers (AMMs): algorithms to handle trades between specific currency pairs. These AMM algorithms take current pricing data from multiple sources (see the chapter on oracles) and use it to price buy or sell requests. They have a price-elasticity curve built in and so if you attempt to buy a lot of a particular asset, the AMM will quote you a higher price.

Over the years, AMMs have become rather sophisticated. For example, with price elasticity curves, the definition of "a lot" depends on the particular asset and how extensively traded it is. High liquidity assets have low "slippage" in price, even with relatively large buy or sell orders. The AMMs also draw upon a pool of liquidity to execute trades since blockchains are not real-time systems and don't really support a model where buyers and sellers are matched dynamically.

Custody Controversy

"Not your keys, not your crypto" is a phrase you will often hear in the world of cryptocurrency and digital assets, most often from "hard core OGs" who have the technical sophistication to feel comfortable holding their own digital assets. Custody services are controversial because they are at odds with the decentralization and individual empowerment ethos in the blockchain ecosystem.

And many of the crypto hard-liners have a good point. Over the years, many exchanges have suffered from poor or corrupt management. When they are not being hacked, centralized exchanges have a long and sad history of acting like banks rather than custody agents and either straight-up stealing their customers' assets or losing them through incompetence. Over time, however, the quality of management has generally improved (though not in all cases) and today you can find well regulated, professionally run and externally audited exchanges with low risks.

Hard-core crypto-types tend to gloss over stories of people who are unprepared for the responsibility of self-custody and lose their money when they leave their hard drive somewhere or forget their private keys. The truth is that very few people or firms are well equipped to manage their own money this way. Indeed, I know many "OGs" in the crypto space (me included) who have been robbed or hacked at one time or another.

What's scary about the world of digital assets is that there's no lender or central authority with the power to "make things right" in the event of a hack or a theft. As a result, losses from theft in many cases cannot be made right. There is no helpdesk that can reset passwords or refill accounts. This means the stakes in the world of digital assets are relatively high, at least when it comes to cryptocurrency.

I would recommend that, unless you are a financial institution with extensive experience in cybersecurity, that it's preferable to work with a reputable custody service and exchange rather than trying to roll your own. Over time, the rate at which exchanges and custody providers are being hacked has gone down significantly, according to Chainalysis, a crypto-analytics company. Advanced mathematics (like multiparty computation – a.k.a. MPC) enables firms to replicate many of the features of centralized systems (password resets!) in a decentralized architecture.

Case Example: Coinbase

Coinbase is one the largest centralized exchanges in the world and the only exchange that is SEC-regulated and publicly traded (on Nasdaq). Coinbase was started in San Francisco in 2012 by Brian Armstrong and Fred Ehrsam, getting some initial seed funding from Y Combinator and in 2013, a series A investment from Union Square Ventures. The company grew rapidly and went public in an IPO in 2021.

Coinbase is subject to perhaps more regulatory scrutiny and disclosure than just about any other exchange out there. As part of the process of going public, the firm was subjected to extensive diligence work around business controls and audit readiness. Coinbase today is audited by Deloitte and publishes audited financial results.

In general, being publicly traded, subjected to SEC regulations and disclosure rules, and professionally audited, should be key requirements in identifying a low-risk exchange and custody partner. Coinbase is the only pure-play in this category in the U.S., but there are a number of other highly regulated entities that offer crypto services to both individuals and enterprises including PayPal, Fidelity, and others.

Case Example: Uniswap

Uniswap is by far the most successful and well-known decentralized exchange. In 2018, Hayden Adams quit his day job as a mechanical engineer at Siemens to pursue his passion and interest in crypto and decentralized systems full-time. The first version of Uniswap went live in 2018.

Unlike Coinbase or other centralized exchanges, Uniswap is just software that exists only on-chain (initially just Ethereum and later other blockchains as well). Uniswap pioneered the use of Automatic Market Makers (AMMs) and liquidity pools to enable transaction matching on-chain without any centralized interference.

In keeping with the fully decentralized ethos of the original vision, Uniswap smart contracts are themselves open-source and the smart contracts are deployed irrevocably on-chain. Uniswap cannot upgrade, or change those contracts, once they are deployed. Instead, over time, Uniswap has deployed updated contracts. As of this writing, Uniswap is on V3 of its DEX smart contract.

The Uniswap software has been used as the foundation for numerous other online decentralized exchanges that have all tried to improve upon the original version, with some success. Uniswap remains the single largest DEX, often executing more than $1 billion in trades every 24 hours. As of November 2022, this was still about 300% larger than the nearest competitor.

Design Considerations and Limitations

For nearly all enterprises transacting in the Ethereum ecosystem, having a centralized exchange relationship will be essential. Beyond the on-off ramp for fiat to crypto and digital assets, however, enterprises will have a choice about how they interact with exchanges and custody providers.

Decentralized exchanges have a relatively small share of the total exchange volume, estimated to be about 10-15% of the market. Decentralized exchanges are very popular with crypto-purists who believe strongly in the decentralized nature of the system beyond Know-Your-Customer and Anti-Money-Laundering controls. I expect, over time, however, that identification and other regulatory compliance aspects will be implemented in these decentralized systems as well.

As the risk that centralized exchanges and custody providers will be hacked has declined, the risk of choosing one of these has also declined. The more public and regulatory scrutiny to which an exchange or custody provider is subjected, the less likely a client is to be in for a nasty surprise. Over the last decade, the business of exchanges and custody have slowly evolved from novel "art" to well-established "science" where best practices and good procedures drive down risk.

The biggest downside of working with centralized exchanges is that the lowest-risk operators are also the most difficult to deal with. They are heavily scrutinized by a large number of regulators, many of which still have widely disparate requirements and expectations. This can make on-boarding as a client or asking them to do new things with real world assets quite challenging.

Decentralized exchanges can work with any standardized fungible token and, increasingly, with non-fungible and hybrid tokens as well. The biggest risk around decentralized exchanges is that regulators remain unsure of how to handle them. Their decentralized nature means that, in theory, there's no central party to hold accountable for results, KYC or AML. In practice, nearly all the decentralized exchanges are maintained and updated by companies that are affiliated with the protocols.

Future Paths

It is sometimes said that organizations that oppose each other also come to resemble each other. This is often true about competition and that looks increasingly to be the case in the world of financial services. While traditional crypto exchanges and custody providers are working to get banking licenses, traditional securities firms and banks are working hard to get into crypto, with the blessing and approval of their regulators.

While this process will take time, over the next few years, it's likely that these two ecosystems will increasingly converge and that most banks will offer features of centralized crypto exchanges and most crypto firms will offer banking functionality, so in time enterprise users will be spoiled for choice.

Implementation Considerations

This is written for enterprises looking for exchange and custody services, not to become exchange or custody providers.

1. What specific services are required?
   a. Exchange (between what and what)
   b. Custody
   c. Access to/from the existing banking system
2. How much regulatory complexity is likely to be involved?
   a. For financial services, likely to be high
   b. For simpler things like inventory management or asset tracking, likely to be low
   c. The greater the importance of regulatory compliance, the more valuable high profile, highly regulated entities provide those services
3. How do you plan to interact with your custody provider and exchange?
   a. Manually with careful handling for one-off transactions?
   b. Automated – connecting it to your ERP or transaction systems so you can send and receive payments and move assets based on

system activity?

    c.   Do you need API access for direct integration / programming?

4.   How valuable are the financial assets involved?

    a.   Just keeping a small amount of Eth to cover transactions costs is a low risk strategy?

    b.   Keeping significant payment volume (>$1 million) or holding assets and investment assets (>$10 million) implies high levels of risk in picking the right custody partner?

    c.   Are the digital assets you are holding just representations of real world assets (e.g. if the digital asset is stolen you have data problem, not theft major financial loss)? Or are these assets valuable directly – in which case securing them becomes important?

BIBLIOGRAPHY

https://twitter.com/ahkek4. "CEX vs DEX Comparison." Dune Analytics. Accessed March 3, 2023. https://dune.com/ahkek/cex-vs-dex-volume-comparison.

Shimron, Leeor. "DEXs Gain Market Share As Faith In Centralized Crypto Players Erodes." *Forbes*, November 23, 2022. https://www.forbes.com/sites/leeorshimron/2022/11/23/dexs-gain-market-share-as-faith-in-centralized-crypto-players-erodes/?sh=5a933c803f40.

"Uniswap (V3) Market Capitalization." Coinmarketcap.com. Accessed March 3, 2023. https://coinmarketcap.com/exchanges/uniswap-v3/.

Yuen, Lo, and Francesca Medda. "Uniswap and the Rise of the Decentralized Exchange." *Munich Personal RePEc Archive*, November 3, 2020. https://mpra.ub.uni-muenchen.de/103925/1/MPRA_paper_103925.pdf.

CHAPTER 23

Decentralized Finance

There are few opportunity spaces that are more compelling and valuable than the space of decentralized finance (DeFi) for Ethereum. The concept behind DeFi is that you can break up the elements of banking and financial services into their core components and then turn them into highly efficient pieces of software code. In traditional banking and finance systems, there is a high degree of friction moving assets between products and services and there is also a lot of friction when it comes to introducing new products and services. Ethereum enables standardization through tokens and smart contracts, improving interoperability. The permissionless and decentralized nature of Ethereum also means that users, not banks, can decide when and how to move their assets.

People love to hate on DeFi, and for good reason. Enormous parts of the DeFi ecosystem are reasonably described as frauds and much of what happened during the crypto boom in 2020 and 2021 can be characterized as "shitcoins" financing each other in an endless meaningless circle of stupid. How was it possible that you could earn 10% interest on your DeFi account but only 0.5% at the bank? The secret ingredient, it turns, was fraud all along. No magical new source of return had been discovered.

In addition to being a giant machine designed to separate rubes from their money, DeFi also turned out to be an amazing tool for theft and money laundering. Sloppy deployment of smart contracts and insider coding (a kind of digital variation on insider trading) made it possible for people to siphon millions, and sometimes hundreds of millions of dollars, from the ecosystem and then launder it through anonymous money mixing services. Great work if you can get it.

On top of all of this, DeFi services turned out to be terrible at regulatory compliance. There are three foundational sets of rules around banking regulations that were largely ignored by DeFi startups. These are Know Your Customer regulations (KYC) that require companies to know with whom they are doing business, and why; Anti-Money-Laundering regulations (AML) designed to prevent you from taking in stolen money and returning money that looks like legitimate profits; and basic risk management, which is intended to prevent customers from signing up for risks they do not really understand.

Maybe, however, it's not fair to say that DeFi services were terrible at regulatory compliance since there's no evidence most of them were ever trying.

DeFi wouldn't be the first industry to get started as a giant violation of the rules, though, and that's not a good reason to throw away what is an immensely useful and innovative idea. Ride-sharing, music downloads, and streaming video all basically started as fairly blatant circling of rules that were in place in different cities, countries, and industries. The value proposition of DeFi isn't just that it's cheap and convenient to break the rules. It's also immensely valuable to be able to decompose many complex services into pieces of code and allow customers to snap them together as they need them.

One of the big attractions of DeFi services, and the reason it grew so quickly in the world of blockchain, is that it makes use of two things that Ethereum does really well: digitization of an asset, and programmability. Since money and money-like digital assets were already digitized, adding programmability was easy to do.

Many basic banking and financial functions can be implemented in an automated manner using smart contracts. For example, a routine banking function is to take assets as deposits and pay interest on those assets. In theory at least, this is pretty simple code to write. Similarly, if you have an asset and you want to borrow against the value of the, it should also be easy to deposit an asset as collateral and then borrow against the value of that asset.

Since digital assets are constantly being traded, in theory, you know what the price of that asset is at any given moment. If borrowers miss a repayment deadline, or the value of the collateral falls below the amount being borrowed, it should be easy, theoretically, to automatically sell those assets into a highly liquid, digital marketplace.

Basically, with a few lines of code, you can build all the key aspects of a bank pretty quickly. But, in practice, running a bank is hard. And, it seems, the DeFi industry decided to "speed run" the entire history of why we have financial regulations in just a few short years. It turns out there are three big problems.

First, in a purely digital environment which does not yet have any structured, standardized model for digital identity, you are, of course, skipping the whole "Know Your Customer" part of the regulations. This means you're quite possibly accepting stolen money and "laundering" it through your "banking" system.

Secondly, it turns out that it's quite easy to manipulate the prices of block-chain-based digital assets. The market may look big, but it is often not very deep. Study after study has found that quite a bit of activity in the crypto eco-system is "wash trading" – that is, people buying and selling to and from them-selves or related entities for the purpose of establishing misleading prices for digital assets.

Third, blockchain markets are very volatile and closely digitally-linked, which makes the possibility of systemic market melt-downs quite possible. Lots of collateralized lending services presented themselves as being safe by limiting the loan-to-collateral value ratios to 70%. That's probably fine in slower-moving, more traditional and liquid markets like real world housing, where gains of 10% or losses of 10% represent major changes in the market, and those often take a year or more to shake out. In the world of crypto, it's routine for tokens to shoot up in value by hundreds of percent, and even more common for them to plunge in value by 90% or more.

And, in the world blockchain, all these markets are digitally intercon-nected in near-real-time. It's quite easy to imagine how a plunge in the value of one asset could trigger automated selling of collateral leading to a cascade of collapses. Normally, plunges in value bring out bargain hunters, but if the process happens too quickly, there may not be time for people to examine the buying opportunity.

The Case for DeFi

There are so many problems with DeFi as it exists today that it can be hard for people to see the value proposition. But there is one, and it's very big. I believe that DeFi will do to banks and finance what app stores did for the software business (and to mobile carriers). It will lead to the componentization of fi-nance and create an entirely new and more competitive industry.

To understand the implications, it's useful to think of another industry analogy: the impact of "Over The Top" (OTT) media streaming on the cable and wireless industry. Prior to the emergence of app stores and smartphones in the 2000s, network operators in both the wired and wireless worlds had a lock on how you consumed digital media. You had to purchase packages of channels or content from the network operator. In the early days of advanced digital mobile phones, network operators were so powerful, they blocked the use of GPS functions unless customers paid extra for a navigation feature and fought against the inclusion of WiFi in new phones, because they could not earn revenue from WiFi data.

Apple shattered all the rules of telecom networks by cutting a five-year exclusive deal with AT&T for the launch of the iPhone in 2007, getting a WiFi-enabled smart device with a browser and, eventually, an App Store, into the hands of millions. Between widespread smart device ownership and the rise of digital piracy, entertainment companies decided that the best path forward was to start offering digital users what they wanted in a reasonably-priced legal package. Streaming services like Hulu were set up in the same year (2007) as the iPhone. Cable companies and wireless network operators started to refer to these internet-based smart-device enabled content services as "Over The Top" services because they bypassed the traditional sales and delivery infrastructure.

The result has been nearly 15 years of slow but steady "cord-cutting" with millions of customers slowly migrating from bundled and packaged pay-TV services towards a-la-carte selections of channels and content delivered over the internet. Pay television subscriptions in the U.S. peaked in 2012 and have been declining at around 7% a year since then. By 2026, it's estimated that pay TV subscriptions will be half of their peak.

I believe this is the future that DeFi has in-store for banking. Just like streaming media, much of DeFi started out as a blatantly illegal software hack on the financial system that appeals to nerds. But the idea of just paying for what you want, and having it delivered how you want, is actually pretty reasonable. Just like the way in which digital media went from illegal hacking to structured, legal streaming services, we can look forward to a future of digital financial services that are delivered a-la-carte through software code, all with full regulatory compliance.

If the world of DeFi was solely about fraud, it would probably never have generated over 1,000 applications in just a couple of years. For a time in 2019-2021, the "giant sucking sound" you could hear on Wall Street was the sound of talented finance professionals walking out of big firms and joining DeFi startups. These startups are interesting for finance professionals because they strip out a lot of complexity that exists in the banking system around risk-management, regulatory compliance and process design and let developers revert to original principles of the financial service.

Eventually, even as the regulatory process gets added back in, there's a good chance that it will be done on a brand-new, fully digital, and completely modern foundation. The result is that even fully-regulated DeFi companies are likely to be much more streamlined and efficient operators than traditional banks. Adding new processes is much easier than figuring out which old ones should be deleted. Large, legacy organizations have many advantages in terms of customer base and process knowledge, but they struggle to know when and how to streamline processes.

Major Types of DeFi Applications

There are 32 different categories of DeFi protocols that have been identified so far and probably in excess of 1,000 different specific applications and offerings, far too many to cover in any substantial way. What I will do here is attempt to go through brief explanations of the top categories.

Decentralized exchanges (DEXs): There are over 600 of these. They are both simple and extremely powerful and widely used. These are just pieces of on-chain software that allow users to buy and sell digital tokens with each other. Although the concept is simple, execution on-chain is complex because blockchains are not real-time systems, they are batch systems. As a result, buying and selling is done asynchronously and algorithms have to estimate how much the price of an asset may change based on your buy or sell order. The biggest decentralized exchange, Uniswap, has paid over $1 billion in fees and dividends back to participants and capital providers so far.

Lending services: These are almost entirely focused on a specific type of lending: collateralized lending where the person wishing to borrow must deposit some collateral against which to borrow. These services compete on offering lower interest rates or higher loan-to-value ratios. AAVE is one of the biggest lending services on-chain and one of the few that offers a regulated sub-pool for identified business users.

Liquid staking: Many protocols require users and participants to put up a stake – basically a "good behavior" bond in order to receive dividends from the transaction fees generated in the system. One problem for some users is that if your token is locked in a good behavior bond, can you do anything else with the capital at the same time? The answer is "yes" with a liquid staking service. The liquid staked token has a value based on the value of the main token and therefore creates the risk that it might be forfeited for bad behavior.

Bridge protocols: These have become both very important and very controversial in recent years. Bridges connect one protocol or blockchain to another by taking a deposit in one protocol and locking that token and then creating a matching token on another protocol. A good example of this is a Bitcoin-to-Ethereum bridge. In the Bitcoin system, a company takes Bitcoin tokens and holds on to them. They create an exactly matching the "wrapped bitcoin" token on Ethereum. You can then transact with the wrapped bitcoin on Ethereum and treat it as, in effect, having the same value as any other bitcoin. This is very popular since there aren't any DeFi services (that I know of) lending on Bitcoin.

The danger here, of course, is that if the two sides get out of sync, you have a lot of risk. What happens if your bitcoin on the Bitcoin blockchain is stolen

– is your wrapped bitcoin no longer having any value. And, what if you borrowed money against your wrapped bitcoin that no longer has any value? It turns out that bridge hacks are a major problem in DeFi with hundreds of millions being stolen and many users losing their money.

Yield and yield Aggregators: Yield services manage the staking of tokens in protocols and collection of rewards, and yield aggregators will distribute your funding across multiple staking protocols.

Derivatives and Options: Just like real world derivatives and options, you can make big bets with leverage or purchase the right to buy or sell assets at a fixed price in the future. The only difference is that this relates to digital tokens instead of traditional stocks and bonds. Given the volatility involved in digital assets adding leverage seems, to put it mildly, risky.

Insurance: This is one of the most innovative and useful categories. Organizations like Nexus Mutual allow people to buy insurance against the risk of smart contract failure or other types of on-chain (and sometimes off-chain) risk.

Anonymity services: These services, most prominently Tornado.Cash allow people to wash their funds through a giant mixing system, making it difficult to track who put money in and who took it out and where. While these services can indeed make your funds and history hard to trace, since Ethereum is a public blockchain, you cannot hide it if you sent or received funds through this service. Sending or receiving money through an anonymity service is an excellent way to get very specific and personalized attention from regulators and tax authorities. Sanctions against Tornado.Cash developers are example of this. It may also make it difficult to get your money out through regulated exchanges, which use analytics tools to block wallets with extensive exposure to these kinds of services.

Real-world assets (RWAs): These are protocols designed to let you link and tokenize assets in the off-chain world (say an office building) and then transact upon them in the Ethereum DeFi ecosystem. This is still a nascent segment and regulations are not at all clear, but over time, this is a strong future use case of decentralized finance – the programmability and automation of financial services based on assets that exist off-chain.

Future Path

If a financial service exists in the real world, it will, sooner or later, have its analog in the world of DeFi. The purpose of DeFi isn't really to recreate existing financial services so much as it is to allow users to mix, edit and adjust their particular approach easily and automatically. There are already on-chain index funds that are designed to help users build portfolios of assets with higher returns and reduced risks.

The biggest and most urgent task of the DeFi sector is to find a scalable, open approach to regulatory compliance. Know Your Customer rules are a good example. Every bank and financial institution is responsible for this on their own, yet there are virtually no industry-wide systems for identifying customers and customer identity data isn't portable from one bank to another. This makes sense if you want to lock in customers for a particular project, but it won't scale up for a decentralized digital finance industry.

As I write this book, a dozen different identity and verification services are being developed by startups that will allow users to take their credentials anywhere and instantly provide proof of identity and the history of their funds and assets. One area where a lot of innovation is happening is around the idea of using Zero-Knowledge Proofs to allow people to prove identity, citizenship, and other data such as sources of funds with a mathematical proof of regulatory compliance rather than the actual data. This preserves privacy while proving compliance.

Blockchain software developers, however, have run far ahead of what users and regulators are able to really understand, absorb, and consider. It will take several years for these regulations to mature. Until then, DeFi will largely be the province of high net-worth individuals and family offices that are allocating a very small share of their assets to test in a high innovation, high risk and high reward ecosystem. DeFi peaked at around $1 trillion in value and collapsed significantly in late-2022 and 2023. Global stock markets alone are worth more than $100 trillion.

Eventually, the hundreds of trillions of dollars in global capital will start to flood into the DeFi ecosystem, as rules and regulations become clear and programmable digital financial services evolve from bug-ridden experiments to hardened scalable systems. It will happen, but not overnight.

Implementation Considerations

1. What is the value proposition for the financial service?
2. What is the asset base on which this service is being built?
    a. On chain or off-chain?
    b. Crypto or stablecoins?
3. What are the key forms of risk in this approach and how can they be managed?
    a. Test and model risk?
    b. Acceptable level of risk?

    c.   Handle extreme market volatility?

4. How will regulatory rules be implemented and enforced?

    a.   KYC?

    b.   AML?

    c.   Security / Offering / Regulatory body?

    d.   Investor accreditation?

5. Who externally is looking at the risks and processes of this entity?

    a.   SOC compliance?

    b.   Code Audits?

    c.   Business Audits?

    d.   Offchain linkages?

6. What external data is needed and used in this system? What kinds of risks are created with these data sources? (Oracles)

    a.   Required?

    b.   Security / services?

7. How does the DeFi protocol govern itself? Are there conflicts between users and "owners" or "stakeholders"?

    a.   Corporation?

    b.   DAO?

    c.   Etc.?

BIBLIOGRAPHY

Defillama. (n.d.). Top Protocols. Retrieved March 19, 2023, from https://defillama.com/top-protocols

AlixPartners. (2021, November 16). Cutting the Cord: How to Compete in a Shifting Ecosystem. Retrieved March 19, 2023, from https://insights.alixpartners.com/post/102hn46/cutting-the-cord-how-to-compete-in-a-shifting-ecosystem

Levy, S. (2008, February 5). The Untold Story: How the iPhone Blew Up the Wireless Industry. Wired. Retrieved March 19, 2023, from https://www.wired.com/2008/01/ff-iphone/

Chainalysis. (2022, February 23). 2022 Crypto Crime Report Preview: NFT Wash Trading and Money Laundering. Retrieved March 19, 2023, from https://blog.chainalysis.com/reports/2022-crypto-crime-report-preview-nft-wash-trading-money-laundering/

Chen, D. K. (2022, February 18). NFT Wash Trading Skyrocketed 700% in 2021, Report Says. The Defiant. Retrieved March 19, 2023, from https://thedefiant.io/nft-wash-trading-2022

Fryer, R. G., Levitt, S. D., List, J., & Sadoff, S. (2021). Enhancing the Efficacy of Teacher Incentives through Loss Aversion: A Field Experiment (No. w30783). National Bureau of Economic Research. Retrieved March 19, 2023, from https://www.nber.org/system/files/working_papers/w30783/w30783.pdf

There's No Future for DeFi Without Regulation

Paul Brody & Rodney Ramcharan

America's first experiment with DeFi didn't end well and the second one is going badly, too. Can we learn the lessons of history to make the third try a success?

Believe it or not, the blockchain era is really America's second experiment with decentralized finance (DeFi). Long before blockchains, the U.S. was the very last of the major industrial countries to establish a central bank. The Federal Reserve System was created in 1913, more than a century after the Bank of England was established and most big European countries had their own central banks as well. Even then, the Fed was established somewhat reluctantly after a series of financial crises.

Prior to the establishment of the Federal Reserve, banking in the U.S. operated like DeFi does today: a kind of "Wild West" with little regulation and no lender of last resort. As a result, a crisis at one bank could quickly lead to contagion at others. The specific crisis that triggered the creation of the Federal Reserve came from a highly leveraged short squeeze that went wrong, leaving the financing company, the Knickerbocker Trust, illiquid. Knickerbocker's collapse led to a broader stock market plunge and a wave of bank runs.

As in 1913, the idea that regulators had a role to play wasn't necessarily popular with everyone. The argument then, as it is now, is the same: Bank crises are painful, but they are a form of market discipline, and crypto ecosystems, because they lack central banks, offer a higher standard of discipline and performance.

Crypto was supposed to be better than 19th century banks. The extreme transparency that blockchain technology enables should have made it clear which funds and firms were operating on the edge, exposed to risky products.

Originally published in CoinDesk in September 2022, reprinted with permission.

Four factors came together to make it hard for a transparent, disciplined market to emerge.

First, many companies and protocols have started to blend on-chain DeFi with off-chain but still unregulated centralized finance (CeFi). Instead of on-chain components that should be clear and transparent, the trail dead-ends in off-chain assets that are unknown or, worse, pledged to multiple owners. If an asset is pledged as collateral on-chain, that's entirely visible to others. If the same asset is pledged off-chain, however, a firm might have liabilities far in excess of what people can determine by looking at on-chain data.

Consequently, if the firm doesn't share that information, assessments made based on-chain data will be dangerously incomplete. Some of this was certainly out-and-out fraud. Much of it was evidence of how badly some firms scaled as they failed to segregate funds or monitor their own processes. It will likely be many months before some of the biggest bankruptcies are fully reported and investigated for us to find out.

Second, transparency has its limits. It's all well and good that fully decentralized and on-chain systems are readable by end users. That doesn't mean end users can understand what they are buying or how to evaluate the risks. Only a tiny fraction of crypto buyers have the technical knowledge (never mind the time) to fully understand the most complex DeFi protocols. In short, as in traditional banking, end users or depositors are dispersed and lack the monitoring expertise to sufficiently discipline these institutions.

Not only are most users not equipped to understand protocols, you cannot have a "flight to quality" without effective benchmarks and other standards for on-chain and off-chain financial services. Banks are subject to liquidity and capital quality standards established by regulators and the results are published.

Finally, markets are not rational in the short run. A speculative frenzy sent everything upwards in the first part of the cycle in early 2021 and despair led people to liquidate quickly in the plunge, which began in November 2021 and continued through much of 2022. Reason may prevail over time, but, in the moment, investors tend not to behave rationally. The automated and interconnected nature of DeFi may accelerate the cascade of panic as well.

It is definitely true that some very well-governed DeFi protocols came through the worst of this crypto winter with little damage. MakerDAO is a good example. Maker – a DeFi lending system that issues the DAI stablecoin – only briefly de-pegged from the dollar and recovered quickly. The other category of firms that have held up well are CeFi firms that have aggressively courted regulators and auditors with an eye on the long game. The reporting rigor required to get a Big 4 auditor or to go public on a U.S. stock exchange is a powerful incentive for organizations.

Maturing the DeFi sector matters because it is the future of banking. And banking crises do much more systematic damage to the economy than other industry problems. The purpose of financial systems is (or should be) to channel capital to firms that make investments and drive productivity and growth in the economy. When they stop working, the effects hit across the whole economy. The 1907 banking crisis in the U.S. led to a decline in industrial production of 11% and a drop in imports of 26%. By way of comparison, this is about the same level of decline that occurred in the global financial crisis in 2008.

While the impact of financial crises may not have changed dramatically before and after the creation of the Federal Reserve, the frequency did. In the 19th century, the U.S. had banking crises and panics in 1819, 1837, 1857, 1873, 1884, 1893 and 1896 – and nearly every one of those led to a recession. In the 20th century, however, we had just one major crisis, the Great Depression. So far in the 21st century, we've also had one major crisis, the Global Financial Crisis, though its impact was far smaller than the Great Depression, thanks to the vision and insights of then-Fed Chair Ben Bernanke.

For blockchain business ecosystems, the lessons are clear: Without embracing regulatory compliance, government-backed insurance models and fiat currencies built atop professionally run central banks have no viable future. Even the best-run firms will not be able to embrace nearly any level of acceptable risk required to produce a decent return or multiply the value of capital. And without that, there's no real future for DeFi.

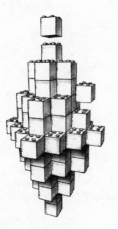

Rodney Ramcharan is a professor of finance and economics at the University of Southern California.

CHAPTER 24

Decentralized Autonomous Organizations

Critics of the online economy often complain about how toxic and destructive it has become. Social media is certainly part of that but even in digital markets, many business relationships have become adversarial. One possible reason for this is that users of social media or digital marketplaces don't necessarily have their incentives aligned with the operators of the networks.

Getting more likes, or "hacking the system," pays dividends now and if the ecosystem as whole has been weakened, that cost is borne by other participants or the network owners. The central idea behind a DAO is to build a better organization and operational model for on-chain activities where the principal / agent problem is solved at the onset.

DAO stands for decentralized autonomous organization (DAOs), as they have evolved, appear to have three central features:

Automated execution of core functions. This is the autonomous component of the approach. Most DAOs are built to support, manage, and maintain on-chain protocols that execute activity automatically. This often includes things like trading, data or content distribution.

Transparent, open decision-making. This is the decentralized component of the approach – rather than having a centralized organization control the entity, key decisions are made by participants using governance tokens. Ownership of a governance token gives people the right to vote on a proposed action or change or a way to spend the DAO treasury.

Aligned incentives among participants. The operating models for DAOs are designed to align the incentives so that people who use the system benefit from its success and also have a stake in the system that makes acting destructively against their own interests.

While the original concept around DAOs centered around highly automated and autonomous systems, in practice, DAOs have become a general-purpose system for organizing blockchain-based entities. The largest DAOs have billions in revenue and hold assets in the billions. These DAOs also have full-time developer and management teams. In effect, many DAOs look like an on-chain version of a share-holder-owned corporation, a cooperative or a partnership.

The very first DAO, "The DAO," was launched in April 2016 as an Ethereum-based venture capital fund. People would contribute money to the system and then vote on the preferred investment choices. Within two months, the DAO had raised nearly $150 million in funds and people were starting to debate how to allocate the money to proposed startups and projects. In June of that year, however, a hacker managed to drain about $50 million of the fund, by exploiting a flaw in the governance and management software of the DAO on-chain.

After much debate, the Ethereum blockchain was "forked" and "rolled bac,k" and the stolen money was returned to the original investors. The DAO organization itself quickly unraveled, though the debate over the decision to effectively undo the theft lasted for years. This was the last time that Ethereum executed a hard-fork to undo the result of a hack. (The unfixed original thread of Ethereum continues to this day as "Ethereum Classic," though it has few users.)

Despite the fiasco of The DAO, the concept gained traction and DAOs have since become a typical approach to building on-chain organizations. Today, there are thousands of DAOs, including an entire category of DAOs that are DAO service and operating companies. Some of the most popular DAO categories include:

- **Investment DAOs.** These are similar to the original DAO, aggregating funds and dispersing them to investment candidates.
- **Grant/public service DAOs.** These are, in effect, charities. The biggest one to-date has been the Crypto Relief DAO established by Sandeep Nailwal, the founder of Polygon. Crypto Relief raised nearly $500 million dollars to support people in India recovering from the COVID-19 pandemic.
- **Protocol DAOs.** Protocols like Uniswap, the decentralized exchange service, are among the most successful types of DAOs established and, in many ways, among the most consistent with the original vision. The Protocol, in this case Uniswap, does the "work" of the DAO
- **Services DAOs.** A number of organizations have been started just to serve and automate the creation of DAOs, both as consulting firms and as SaaS applications that simplify the interaction with the blockchain.

- **Social DAOs.** Social networks, services, and clubs all funded by and gated through ownership of governance tokens.
- **Media DAOs.** A range of media companies and entities, including the Bankless DAO, have been started and funded in the DAO model.

In essence, the universe of DAOs looks like any other startup or business ecosystem.

Business Value Proposition

The value proposition of DAOs basically mimics any other business ecosystem, except that it moves the core infrastructure of ownership and management on-chain. DAOs have a few advantages:

1. **Community engagement.** In most DAOs, individual holders of governance tokens can propose plans and debate actions and then get them submitted to a vote of the token holders. Although only a minority of token holders typically engage, rates of engagement are typically higher than with shareholder votes in traditional publicly-held enterprises. Some DAOs, such as Nouns DAO (Nouns.wtf), are renowned for their high levels of engagement.

2. **Automated governance logic.** While any traditional enterprise can set up and get approved rules defining how owners can engage or interact with the company they own, those all have to be implemented manually. DAOs can set up and execute automated business logic with on chain governance rules. This includes features like the ability to delegate authority on voting to others and concepts like quadratic voting which limit the power of any one holder to dominate the system.

3. **Operational transparency.** Where more traditional businesses may report limited information periodically, such as quarterly, DAOs offer extraordinarily high levels of transparency to end users, including detailed information (for those willing to dig through it) on how all the money is being spent.

4. **Incentive alignment.** DAOs often require users to hold and stake tokens in the system. The nearest real-world analogy here is that of a cooperative or a partnership: behavior and incentives are aligned because the system's users are also the system's owners.

Although DAOs can be organized to act as traditional businesses, they are especially well suited to more cooperative ventures like charities, public services, cooperatives, and partnerships which depend upon engagement with a community to be successful.

Case Example: MakerDAO

MakerDAO is one of the oldest and widely regarded as among the best-run DAOs on-chain. MakerDAO is responsible for the Dai digital asset, which is a U.S.-dollar-pegged digital asset on the Ethereum blockchain. It's often described as an multi-collateralized stablecoin to distinguish it from more traditional stablecoins that are backed by actual U.S. dollars (or other fiat currencies.).

Dai tokens are generated as a loan against crypto-assets. Initially the only acceptable crypto-asset was Ether and later on more and more assets were accepted. Most of these loans are over-collateralized, so that the system can handle ups and downs in the price of Ether without losing the U.S. dollar peg. As of January 2023, there were about $5 billion in Dai operating on the Ethereum blockchain, making it by far the biggest and most successful multi-collateral stablecoin.

The website forum.makerdao.com hosts extensive discussions over proposals to be voted on by the community. The website vote.makerdao.com provides frontend access to voters for casting their lots on these proposals by using voting power in the form of MKR tokens. Some are very detailed and technical, covering specifics of new assets or proposals to develop code extensions. Others are focused on business goals and metrics.

One proposal that was debated and passed in 2021 was a plan to terminate the MakerDAO content production team. The proposal came from a member of the community who was engaged in promoting Maker. He felt like community members often did a better job than the paid-up members of the marketing team. The proposal was hotly debated, but eventually passed 49.1% to 47.3%, resulting in the immediate termination of that team.

MakerDAO is widely considered a benchmark in the world of Ethereum for stability and transparency in the governance model. Rune Christensen, the founder, has played a big role in decentralizing the service and building a robust community. Though he still has significant influence, much of the hard work of leadership and engagement comes from the community members.

Case Example: Gitcoin

Gitcoin started in 2017 as an idea by Kevin Owocki to try to solve two problems: how to find talented engineers (without paying exorbitant headhunter fees) and how to fund open-source software projects that serve the public good. Ethereum incubator ConsenSys funded the early start for Gitcoin and the organization spun out with investment from Paradigm in January 2021. In May, Gitcoin officially became a DAO. The goal of the Gitcoin DAO is now to empower communities to build and fund what matters to them.

The need for structured public service investment tools is high. Like the internet and much of civil society, the Ethereum ecosystem may support trillions in commerce and value, but it is in fact sustained in many key areas by volunteer efforts. Sometimes, critical projects and infrastructure fall through funding gaps despite being enormously important. OpenSSL, the internet security tool that much of the internet depends upon, is maintained by a small foundation with just two full time employees scraping by. The "Heartbleed" bug in 2011 left two-thirds of the web vulnerable to hacking briefly due to an avoidable error in the SSL code that would likely have been caught with better funding and staffing.

The main product today of the Gitcoin DAO is the Gitcoin grants protocol, Allo. The system is designed to help people organize and manage public funding initiatives. Funding grants are done in rounds every three months and money for these projects come from two sources: larger program donors and individual contributors. Project operators submit proposals for grants and they ask individual contributors to donate to projects through the platform. Small donations are then matched by a distribution of funds from the larger program donors.

One key innovation that Gitcoin is pioneering "quadratic funding." This uses a mathematical formula that is designed to balance decision-making power between large numbers of small donors and small numbers of big donors. Instead of just matching individual donor grants one for one, this formula gives significant weight to individual contributors, regardless of their funding amount on the grounds that this is a good measure of likely project impact and adoption. This arguably makes quadratic funding the most democratic method of distributing capital.

As of writing, Gitcoin has distributed more than $50 million across 105 Quadratic Funding pools, facilitating over 3.7 million supporter-grantee transactions. it has become one of the most highly regarded public service entities in the world of Ethereum.

Limitations and Solution Design Considerations

DAOs are an incredibly flexible and useful way to establish an organization onchain. There are perhaps two major risks involved in setting up and running a DAO. The first is software risk: just like the original DAO, entities that are based on code are hackable. As the space has matured, the risks associated with this have declined but not disappeared.

The second big risk is around the regulatory landscape. There's limited legal recognition for DAOs and in some cases, the operation of a DAO looks so much like a shareholder-owned company, it is almost certainly likely to fall afoul of securities laws. Charities, cooperatives, and privately run companies by qualified investors are probably in much better shape, but the space is too new and there are far too few explicit rules for firms to be sure. Some states in the U.S., like Texas and Wyoming have passed laws allowing DAOs to register themselves as LLCs. Any company should consult their legal counsel before setting up a DAO.

Beyond the risk-related limitations, there are a host of design decisions that firms must make in the process. At the highest level, while there are many good guides for how to effectively run and manage publicly traded and systematically audited firms, not many firms have adapted them to the DAO process and structure. As a result, there's more work for people to do building up and implementing generally recognized good governance processes.

Future Paths

DAOs need increased legal clarity and status. Beyond that, there are a number of frontiers where DAOs can mature significantly. One area is enabling different levels of privacy within the system. EY built a private voting system for a DAO in 2022 and other types of selective privacy might be used to encourage participation or protect emerging business secrets without damaging the fundamental principles of openness. Audits by professional firms and standardized governance models would also go a long way to reducing risk and complexity in the space.

Implementation Considerations

1. What is the purpose and membership of this organization?
    a. Who is joining?
    b. What is the purpose of the organization?
    c. What problem are you solving and is a DAO a good fit for a cooperative development model?
2. How will the organization be funded and who will the staking model work to incentive constructive participation?
    a. How is the initial funding made?
    b. Who are the stakeholders in this business and what priority/accountability do they have over each other?
        i. Tokenholders
        ii. Shareholders

        iii.   Others

    c.   Will users/members need to stake (lock up their tokens) in order to use the system?

    d.   If there are pay-outs, how will they be made? Based on ownership? Participation?

3.   What will the decision-making process be within the organization?

    a.   Voting mechanism and system?

    b.   Voting algorithm (shares, votes, quadratic)?

4.   What real-world traditional regulatory structure will the organization make use of?

    a.   Corporation, LLC, Coop, DAO?

    b.   National jurisdiction?

5.   How will the economic incentives or token incentives of the organization be implemented?

    a.   What will the primary means of exchange be in this system? Is there a value capture mechanism to sustain the organization?

        i.   DAO or protocol Token-based

        ii.   Dollar-based

        iii.   Eth-based

        iv.   Other?

BIBLIOGRAPHY

"1InchDAO Governance." Accessed February 19, 2023. https://1inch.io/dao/.

Buterin, Vitalik, Zoe Hitzig, and E. Glen Weyl. "A Flexible Design for Funding Public Goods." *ArXiv*, August 16, 2020. https://arxiv.org/pdf/1809.06421.pdf.

The Economist. "Coase's Theory of the Firm," July 29, 2017. https://www.economist.com/schools-brief/2017/07/29/coases-theory-of-the-firm.

Explain XKCD. "Dependency," August 17, 2020. https://www.explainxkcd.com/wiki/index.php/2347:_Dependency.

Falkon, Samuel. "The Story of the DAO - It's History and Consequences." *The Startup* (blog), December 24, 2017. https://medium.com/swlh/the-story-of-the-dao-its-history-and-consequences-71e6a8a551ee.

Explain XKCD. "Heartbleed Explanation," April 11, 2014. https://www.explainxkcd.com/wiki/index.php/1354:_Heartbleed_Explanation.

"Nouns History." Accessed February 19, 2023. https://nouns.center/history.

"Welcome to Syndicate." Accessed February 19, 2023. https://guide.syndicate.io/en/getting-started/welcome-to-syndicate.

Gitcoin Support. "What Is the Gitcoin Grants Program." Accessed February 19, 2023. https://support.gitcoin.co/gitcoin-knowledge-base/gitcoin-grants/what-is-a-grant.

"WTF Is Quadratic Funding." Accessed February 19, 2023. https://wtfisqf.com/.

III.

ADVANCED TOPICS

CHAPTER 25
Introduction to Advanced Topics

Technology ecosystems are immensely complex. What we think is simple builds upon waves of innovation all stacked up on each other. As Ethereum matures, I look forward to an era when many of these "advanced" topics will be so far down the technology stack that we will hardly need to give them any thought.

We're not there yet, however, and so as you go further down the path of implementing or thinking through a solution on Ethereum, it's useful to answer questions that will come up, such as "Is this going to create a big carbon footprint?" or "Why shouldn't we do this on a private blockchain and control it ourselves?" That will help future-proof your strategy.

CHAPTER 26

Tokenomics

Blockchains like Ethereum are a large-scale experiment in digital democracy and commerce. Though blockchains generally, and Ethereum specifically, often seen as an extreme environment of financialization-of-everything, many of the original creators and builders in this ecosystem, myself included, are trying to make a better, fairer world.

In many respects, the economic models that are being implemented in Ethereum are not necessarily new. Many of the protocols, decentralized autonomous entities, and businesses that are being built, are designed at least in part to mimic cooperatives and partnerships in their goals to align incentives and obtain responsible behavior as a result.

You only have to look at the world of media ecosystems to see how people freeride on social media platforms, or even how television networks spread hate or misinformation. These people and corporations generate short-term engagement and profits at the expense of our broader society. Smaller variations of these conflicts seem to exist in nearly every business ecosystem.

What is different in Ethereum is the effort to address these problems with technology and at scale. Though business partnerships and co-ops can become quite large, they are still dwarfed in size and scale by corporations. As organizations get larger, it gets harder and harder to coordinate activities and agreements in a highly democratic manner. Large firms are good at capturing economies of scale, but they're often bad at surfacing and incubating good ideas internally.

Economists talk about the "theory of the firm", and often refer to the work of British Economist Ronald Coase. In the 1930s, Coase wanted to understand why firms exist at all. Shouldn't the market organize everything? It turns out that coordinating activities is costly and complex. Simple, easy-to-define tasks are easily sub-contracted while complex tasks with subjective outcomes are not.

For example: Buying existing batteries is easy for an electric car. Building an entirely new kind of battery and making sure it works with the car design is not. One of these is easy to "externalize" in a contract, the other makes sense to "internalize" as part of an integrated team of scientists and engineers.

In the world of Ethereum, people talk about the "Coordination Problem" but they are, in effect, looking at the same thing. That is, how to get large numbers of people in a distributed global ecosystem to work together for a common good. The result is an entire discipline of tokenomics, the drive to figure out how to design the economic incentives and operating models of the Ethereum ecosystem in a way that results in high levels of constructive coordination.

Herewith, in plain English, is my best effort to explain some of the key concepts and how they work together. It's worth noting that reality falls far short of the ideal. Even worse, scammers and con artists, of which there are plenty in this ecosystem, have ruthlessly exploited these ideas to drive coordinated buying, and then found creative ways to run off with the money. Nonetheless, the commitment to finding a better way to coordinate people and action for public good at scale remains.

Some of the key concepts that are worth understanding are as follows:

Token sales fund protocol development. Token sales by entities effectively look like a form of crowdfunding or an IPO. Indeed, these were often called Initial Coin Offerings, or ICOs. This was perhaps the most widely abused part of the tokenomics ecosystem where people put out ambitious white papers and often raked in hundreds of millions in funding (occasionally billions) and never produced a product.

The concept of crowdfunding as a democratic/market indicator of likely demand is well established, but there's a reason that Silicon Valley VCs hand out relatively small amounts of money at a time: very few products make it from concept to reality. In theory, however, pre-sales of tokens are essential for funding initial product development work.

Protocol development organizations retain tokens as assets. Product development organizations usually only release a small portion of their tokens in the initial funding round. The protocol treasury usually holds on to the rest, releasing them as needed to fund additional development.

Protocol usage generates fees. Once a protocol is up and running, it is usually necessary to pay fees into the system for each transaction. For example, in a decentralized exchange, buyers and sellers usually need to add a small extra fee to cover the transaction cost. That fee goes back to the protocol treasury. Sometimes the fee is paid in the protocol native token and sometimes it is paid in another token. If it's not paid in native token of the protocol, it's almost always paid in Eth or U.S.-dollar-pegged stablecoin.

Protocols pay out to token holders. As protocols become successful and their treasuries start filling up with transaction fees, protocols can then return money to the investors through either token-buy-backs or dividends. (This is theory: there aren't many cases yet of this actually happening.)

Token staking incentivizes good behavior. Users of the protocol are often expected to "stake" native tokens or Eth to participate in a protocol. This is similar to a coop or partnership buy-in that is intended to fund operations and to align incentives. Bad actors who violate protocol rules or hack the system can be "slashed" and lose their stake.

These five components are fairly typical but there is a broad range of variations. People are constantly experimenting with improvements in how to allocate funds and drive incentives.

Coordination Challenges

As wonderful as the idealistic vision is behind the concept of tokenomics, there are a lot of problems that are only being slowly worked out. In fairness, joint stock companies and the like have been evolving since the Dutch East India company issued shares on the Amsterdam stock exchange in 1602. In particular, there are a number of problems that are still being worked through and here are some of the biggest:

Regulatory games. If you read the section above and thought "wow, that looks like an IPO for a company and then a plan to earn money and pay a dividend" you are, in my opinion, right. The SEC feels the same way. Many of these ICOs and tokens are unregistered securities and organizations have tried all kinds of gimmicks and twists like registering off-shore, setting up foundations and related for-profit entities to try to pass themselves off as something else. The presence of big money venture capital instead of charities suggests that's not the case.

Conflicts of interest. Some of the firms that issued tokens in the ICO boom are also shareholder owned corporations. In these cases, which group of "stakeholders" is in charge? It's not hard to see how, in the future, token-holders will have incentive to prefer changes that optimize the total ecosystem while shareholders will prefer those which maximize profit extraction.

Transparent complexity. You will hear blockchain boosters talk endlessly about the elegance and transparency of blockchain-based operations. And, indeed, many of these firms do run extremely transparent operations with published rules and traceable processes. Good luck figuring it all out. A combination of highly complex rules and low investor/user engagement creates an environment that's highly preferential for the needs of insiders.

Every emerging industry is a mess and blockchain has proven to be no exception. Understanding these key concepts (and how they have been misused) will be helpful in evaluating and designing your own tokenomics.

CHAPTER 27
Audits & Verification

The idea behind audits is simple: have a third party evaluate the correctness of an organization's financial statements because people and organizations are not always able to objectively evaluate their own performance or business decisions. Audits emerged in the 19th century as a response to repeated accounting and fraud scandals and the Institute of Chartered Accountants in England and Wales was established in 1880. The ball really got moving during the wave of regulatory activity that took place during the great depression after the stock market crash of 1929. The Securities Act of 1933 required companies to be audited if they were selling shares and the 1934 act required publicly traded companies to file audited financial statements. The rules have only gotten tighter and tougher since then, especially with the arrival of the Sarbanes-Oxley legislation in 2002 that mandated companies to assert the effectiveness of their internal controls and auditors to audit the effectiveness of internal controls over financial reporting.

Though financial statement audits are not officially designed to find fraud so much as they are designed to make sure that assessments are correct and developed using good practices, they make fraud more difficult and often act as a deterrent. There isn't a lot of data from the "before audit" period in the 1800s that allows a rigorous comparison, but there is some strong academic research that shows companies that are audited have less fraud and fewer restatements of accounts, that audit quality is closely aligned with professional standards, and high-quality firms that invest in meeting those professional standards.

As with a lot of emerging businesses, the crypto industry has suffered from a high level of fraud and dishonesty. Not only are many companies completely dishonest, but lots of companies lied or misrepresented by saying they were audited. There is no law that restricts the use of the word audit, and so lots of firms claim to offer audits or have been audited, but it is key to understand what kind of "audit" was actually done, if those audits were conducted in accordance with professional standards, and if there is regulatory power and authority overseeing the work being done. This chapter aims to explain the most common types of professional "assessments" available, how they work, and their limitations.

Financial Statement Audits

When people talk about audits, in general, this is most often what they mean: a financial statement audit. Financial statement audits are done on a periodic basis, usually once a year, and they are designed to make sure that a company is representing their overall financial position, results of operations and cash flows in accordance with Generally Accepted Accounting Principles. This doesn't mean they represent a comprehensive view of everything the company does. However, there is an ongoing drive to make more matters subject to explicit outside assessment, such as internal controls, greenhouse gas emissions, and so forth.

Certified Public Accountants (or the equivalent title outside the United States) are typically regulated at a national level and are generally required under professional standards to be competent, trained, professional, and impartial. This means training, certification, and on-going education. Additionally, regulators require that audit firms maintain a high level of independence from their clients. This typically means that audit firms have limited business relationships with the companies they audit. Rules on auditor independence typically mean that audit firms should not provide certain non-audit services (with exceptions that vary by country) to the firms they audit to avoid a conflict of interest. One key aim is to avoid a situation where auditors might be called upon to evaluate the work of their colleagues in the same firm. Global professional standards are issued by the International Auditing and Assurance Standards Board (IAASB), and every country has its own regulatory specifications as well – most often adaptations of the globally issued standards.

Audits generally involve five major activities, and I will explain them here with crypto-currency and blockchain-specific examples. Because this isn't a book about audit, I'm not going to explain all the nuances involved in these rules. You can, for example, complete an audit without having a full set of business controls if you do substantive testing instead. Entire textbooks have been written on the detailed processes and rules. My goal is rather to explain some key activities and help non-audit businesspeople understand the kinds of things they should be asking about and looking for.

1.   **Assessing Business Controls.** Well run businesses have strong controls in place internally. This includes simple things like not having excessive internal conflicts of interest and basic rules about how high

value items are handled. A good example of this in the world of blockchain is making sure that if you are a crypto-currency exchange, and you are buying and holding assets for your customers, you are not giving those assets to another part of your organization to trade with or borrow against. If your organization has both a trading arm and a deposit arm, you have to make sure that the management team of one cannot pressure the other to share assets or lend money.

2. **Substantive Testing.** This means taking specific data points from internal data and verifying that they are correct and accurate and, when relevant, aligned with the external marketplace. In the case of digital assets, it's very easy to show that there is an on-chain wallet that contains assets, but does your company control it? Can you match the total of all money given to the company to buy digital assets with the total supply of those digital assets? For example, EY's Blockchain Analyzer software is used in the audit process to match up all transactions in a company's internal accounts with their actual transactions on a public blockchain and verify digital signatures on all wallets shown.

3. **Evaluating Judgements & Valuations:** One of the toughest areas in any financial statement audit is evaluating the value of assets and liabilities. Sometimes, such as with highly liquid stocks or bonds, this isn't hard at all. Many times, however, it is highly subjective and open to interpretation. Digital Assets offer some benefits because they can be traded online, but in many cases, liquidity is thin or nonexistent. Are the inputs, assumptions, and logic used by the company to assign a value reasonable?

4. **Assessing Disclosures.** Companies must disclose all substantive risks and complexities associated with their business models. Everyone should read these disclosures, though not all do. For those who take the time, they can be goldmines of accurate and compelling information about these companies and the risks they face. Believe it or not, most airlines routinely warned in their annual report disclosures that a pandemic would crater their business. Cryptocurrency and blockchain companies face all kinds of new and novel risks, including software failures that could prove catastrophic.

5. **Reporting.** All this data has to be packaged together in a standardized way that should make it easy for experienced investors to understand how their investments are performing and, where possible, have somewhat consistent definitions in basic things like revenues, costs, assets and liabilities.

One particular problem with financial statement audits is that they are only done once a year and they represent the finances of a firm, not necessarily the on-chain business operations. To the extent that a firm's finances are directly linked to on-chain transactions, this means there is a close linkage, but financial statement audit should not be taken as an assurance that smart contracts are functioning correctly, for example.

If you're not audited and you want to be audited, especially by a "Big 4" firm like EY, it's important to understand that this isn't a quick or simple process and there's a reason why top-tier auditors turn away many clients. The stakes are very high. Top audit firms place immense value on their reputations. Indeed, there is academic evidence that investors consider firms audited by top tier auditors to be lower risk. Additionally, the penalties for negligence or malpractice can be large enough to end a firm's existence. The Big 4 used to be the Big 5. Even if the penalties aren't firm-ending, they can still be very large. In many countries, it is not permitted for audit firms to limit their liability.

The result of this high-stakes business model is that auditors are cautious about the clients they pick up. Not only are all the senior officers of a prospective client reviewed, but companies must make extensive investments in reporting system and business controls before they can be "accepted" as clients. This is not cheap or fast. Major EY clients in the audit area have often spent two-to-three years and upwards of $10 million doing audit-readiness work to prepare.

Attestation Reports

While financial statement audits are done on an annual basis, attestation reports are reports performed under similar professional standards that can be done as needed and for a specific activity or area. Attestation reports typically have to be signed-off by certified public accountant. There are quite a few different kinds of these reports and none of them carry the same weight as a full audit.

One area that I think will become routine for attestation reports are stablecoins, where banks or stablecoin firms will want to have reporting under professional standards on the amount of reserves supporting a particular digital asset off-chain and how it aligns with the on-chain liabilities.

It's important to note here that "attestation" reports provided by non-Audit firms do not carry the same weight or professional requirements as those that are done by certified public accountants.

Agreed-Upon Procedures (AUPs)

AUP reports are when an auditor performs specific, agreed-upon procedures and generates a report. AUPs are all about testing some specific facts. In the case of blockchain, a fact that might be tested is "did this token get transferred within the agreed upon dates." AUPs, unlike audits, do not have an opinion associated with them, but they do provide an analysis of a specific part of an organization's activities and responsibilities conducted by a third party. So the AUP report on a token transfer would not, for example, make any assessment as to whether or not the price paid for that token is a fair market value. AUPs are often done to analyze a specific element of the business. However, because the scope is "agreed upon" by the engaging party(ies), they can often be unsuitable for third party users.

Systems and Organization Controls Reports (SOC)

In many cases, it is not possible for auditors to feasibly keep track of all information or verify it at all times. Additionally, there are often few choices for data available, so there is no alternative that you have but to trust a single data provider. Though this is not yet widely the case, it is easy to see a future where smart contracts are triggered by external data that is only available from a single supplier. For example, if I have a smart contract and payment is triggered by delivery of the goods, that means I am dependent on the logistics company to report delivery of those goods.

SOC reports provide information on the controls over the data provided by a third party and a means to have evidence of the function of such controls. In this case, auditors cannot verify every shipment and it is not feasible to apply crowdsourcing to delivery data on millions of packages. However, auditors can understand and test the process and controls a company has in place for reporting out this data. Third party service providers can have a SOC engagement performed and provide the report to entities they provide services to and those entities auditors.

SOC reports come in three major "flavors." SOC 1 reports usually concern financial controls while SOC 2 and 3 reports cover security, availability, processing integrity, and privacy business controls. Over time, I expect to see many organizations obtain SOC reports for key parts of their blockchain-related business process.

Smart Contract Audits (Aren't)

One of the most common services offered in the world of blockchain software are Smart Contract Audits. These are generally designed to see if a smart contract functions as expected and is free from major technical errors, bugs, or security weaknesses. In theory, a thoroughly audited smart contract would be much lower risk than one that has not been carefully reviewed and tested.

Unfortunately, these are not audits and should not be treated as such. Indeed, while EY offers services that are very similar to what other companies call "Audits," ours are called "Smart Contract Reviews" for a very good reason: we're not offering any assurance or guarantee that the software is free from bugs. There isn't any known practical way to make such a guarantee. Additionally, there really aren't any globally regulated and widely adopted standards for software verification against which one could objectively compared a particular smart contract.

That is not to say I don't strongly recommend smart contract reviews. I do. And because there isn't any perfect standard for securing smart contracts, the more effort you put into testing and bug hunting, the better. You should get more than one if you're talking about serious money being deployed into these applications or sensitive data, but just understand it's not an audit, and it doesn't come with the kind of rigorous expectations you would have with a globally regulated and standardized audit approach.

Proof of Reserves (Also Not an Audit)

Proof of Reserves is another area that has, at times, been offered by companies operating on Ethereum as evidence of their solvency. The concept behind proof of reserves is that individual users should be able match their account balance at a crypto-exchange with on-chain data and that, as a whole, they should be able to check that, as a whole, the firm they're using has an on-chain balance equal to the amount of their depositor liabilities.

In practice, this doesn't work well and firms that have offered this service have generally stopped doing so. There are two problems that often come up. First, it's technically and mathematically difficult to follow the on-chain and off-chain data verification process. I had some EY R&D staff, people with PhD-level math skills and programming skills, look at cases where they had accounts that offered "Proof of Reserves." In both cases, while they were able to make the numbers "match up," they all found it challenging and time consuming and not particularly comforting. And these are people who have full-time jobs in blockchain and PhD level math skills. If it's this hard for them, it's basically impossible for the rest of us.

Secondly, proof of reserves doesn't take into account the rest of the organization or balance sheet. Yes, the firm might have all that money, but if they have terrible business controls and someone else is borrowing against that money, it's not necessarily all there for the depositor. Proof of Reserves presents only one slice of a total financial statement picture, and it's much too easy to imagine ways to manipulate that data to make the numbers add up.

Trust But Verify

The idea that we can "trust the math" and not worry about the people involved is enchanting, but it has led nowhere. Complex technology systems have unpredictable behaviors, so even if every blockchain investor and user was mathematically sophisticated and technically proficient, we would still face risk. On top of that, we've seen time and again that this is a business with lots of bad actors. In this environment, both for your business partners and your own operations, it's hard to overstate how important multiple layers of external verification and transparency are worth.

Since no one oversight process is perfect, the more transparent and deeply entwined into a regulatory environment a firm is, the better. Being audited is good, but being audited and also regulated by, say the FDIC or the Federal Reserve and the SEC is probably even better. And never ever believe a firm that says their systems are too sophisticated or too complex for an auditor to understand.

SOURCES

Francis, J. R., Maydew, E. L., & Sparks, H. C. (1999). The role of Big 6 auditors in the credible reporting of accruals. Auditing: A Journal of Practice & Theory, 18(2), 17-34. https://doi.org/10.2308/aud.1999.18.2.17

Krishnan, G.V. "Audit Quality and the Pricing of Discretionary Accruals." Auditing: A Journal of Practice & Theory, vol. 22, no. 1, March 2003, pp. 109-126. DOI: 10.2308/aud.2003.22.1.109.

Lennox, C. S. (1999). Audit quality and auditor size: An evaluation of reputation and deep pockets hypotheses. Journal of Business Finance & Accounting, 26(7-8), 779-805. https://doi.org/10.1111/1468-5957.00295

Beatty, Randolph P. "Auditor Reputation and the Pricing of Initial Public Offerings." The Accounting Review, vol. 64, no. 4, 1989, pp. 693-709. JSTOR, www.jstor.org/stable/247856.

CHAPTER 28

Enterprise Adoption Life Cycles

One of the most successful marketing campaigns of the 20th century was the Kodak company's effort to convince consumers to capture life's most memorable and important moments on film. These were known as "Kodak Moments." Kodak was enormously successful and dominated the market for camera film right up until it was replaced by digital cameras in smartphones. Kodak spent a century building an enormous business that collapsed by more than 90% in less than a decade. The story has become a staple of business school classes on disruption.

Stories about collapses like Kodak's are great scare stories but I don't think they're typical of business "disruption." In fact, business disruption is pretty rare. What happens, more often than not, isn't a market collapse but rather a slide into profitable irrelevance. Radio didn't die when TV came along. It's still out there, a very profitable decent business. It's just a fraction of the size of the TV business. As new technologies come along, old ones sediment beneath them, still alive, but no longer growing quickly.

While the most famous stories like this are concentrated in consumer applications, this model of slow phase-out is the typical evolution of an enterprise system. For people trying to build and deploy enterprise systems, the slow pace of enterprise technology adoption can be immensely frustrating. And, while consumers can seemingly adopt new technologies wholesale in around a decade, enterprises seem to take closer to 25-30 years to go from initial application development to the late-adopter stage.

There are several key factors that are responsible for the very slow rate of adoption in large enterprises.

The most important is that enterprise technologies run as systems, not sets of standalone tools and applications. Consumers can add and subtract as they please, but nearly every enterprise system is carefully plugged into sets of input and outputs. The time and money invested in integrating these systems to each other and making sure that workflows through them smoothly is usually greater than the cost of the system itself. In the software business, it's not uncommon to assume $3 of consulting for every $1 of cloud computing or software license fees.

From landline telephones to paper checks, there are more examples than I can count of ways in which business process inertia can slow down adoption of new technology. Enterprises are also slow decision-makers overall. The software license agreements that individual users click on and accept without reading get reviewed and often negotiated extensively at the enterprise level. Pricing, features, and customization all get negotiated as well.

One Killer Application at a Time

Slow though it might be to adopt new technology, the enterprise space does get there eventually. Typically, this happens one "killer application" at a time. The mother of these use cases in information technology might well be the 1890 U.S. Census, which was the first to be tabulated by punch cards. The census was a bonanza for the Hollerith Punch Card Machine Company, eventually to be known as International Business Machines.

IBM repeated this practice of building industry-specific applications time and again. In the late-1950s and 1960s, IBM's industry focus on banking, insurance, and travel all drove waves of adoption. SABRE, the Semi-Automatic Business Research Environment, was the world's first interactive digital airline reservation system, built by IBM for American Airlines on two IBM 7090 Mainframes. IBM still sells about $10-15 billion a year in mainframes and related software and services. The IBM Z-Series mainframe platform is a direct descendent of the System/360, launched in 1964.

Enterprise adoption of PCs started with very specific applications, like Visicalc for spreadsheets, WordPerfect for Word Processing, and Lotus Notes for collaboration. In the mobile phone era, many think of the Blackerry's email service as the tool which pushed smartphones into the enterprise. Eventually, mainframes, PCs and mobile devices moved out of the realm of application-specific tools and started to take on a more general-purpose platform model, as enterprises started to run their entire business models and operations on them and companies developed solutions specifically to take advantage of the presence of these platforms in the hands of consumers and enterprises.

This will be no different in the world of blockchain. Cryptocurrency and NFTs may have been the initial lures for consumers, but now that millions of consumer digital wallets exist in the Web3 space, the user base itself, complete with money and investment interest, is becoming the key driver.

With Web3, cryptocurrencies and NFTs have been enormously popular with consumers, but haven't resonated as much with enterprises, though they are starting to adopt NFTs, primarily as tools for consumer engagement. What has had a big impact is decentralized finance, which has started to make inroads into institutional investors, family offices, and some big banks. Regulatory risk and complexity and the lack of clear rules around the world in finance are slowing adoption, but this is a temporary factor that will resolve with legislation and rulemaking.

Beyond finance, industrial applications are even better candidates for enterprise adoption. No regulatory approvals are needed to manage inventory, track machinery, or manage business contracts. These use cases have not been waiting for a value proposition or a vision, but rather, a practical, scalable implementation. In this case, the missing ingredient was privacy technology that could work on public blockchain, a problem that's now solved, though not yet matured and scaled.

Inflection Points and Adoption Drivers

While it is not hard to envision use cases for blockchain technology, this book is full of them, what matters is not merely showing something is feasible, but also making it work well enough to be practical and showing the world the value proposition. To do that, you need a client that is willing to go first, a solution that creates value, and a path to adoption that's not too onerous. I've identified four key requirements that seem to be needed to go from good ideal to "adoption inflection point":

Better isn't good enough. Merely having a slightly better solution than what is used today isn't good enough to drive adoption. It needs to be substantially better to make the risk involved in a new technology worth the effort. Positive ROI on paper is necessary, but not sufficient.

Upgrades are needed. Companies tend to have an "ain't broke, don't fix it" mentality when it comes to systems. New technologies are often embraced when the existing solution reaches end of life or a manufacturer withdraws support. And sometimes companies seem to wait a few years after that.

Partner onboarding is crucial. Unlike a lot of enterprise systems, blockchains only have value as part of the work for integrating an ecosystem. Whether they are suppliers or customers, companies must be able to bring them into the solution in simple ways, such as simple APIs, Web pages, or even accepting EDI messages.

References are critical. There is no tool for convincing clients that is more important in the enterprise than the referenceable client. Ideally, they need to be in the same industry and even running a similar process to be most compelling.

Finally, when driving adoption of Ethereum, patience will be needed. Enterprises are just not fast movers. Things may go a bit quicker as you get closer to consumers and a bit slower as you move further back in the value chain. But the overall cycle time is always likely to be two-to-three- times longer than with a consumer product business.

BIBLIOGRAPHY

IBM. (n.d.). Sabre. IBM. Retrieved March 19, 2023, from
   https://www.ibm.com/ibm/history/ibm100/us/en/icons/sabre/
IBM. (n.d.). Tabulator. IBM. Retrieved March 19, 2023, from
   https://www.ibm.com/ibm/history/ibm100/us/en/icons/tabulator/
Sauer, T. (2006, April 15). CIOs Sharpen Their Mainframe Exit Strategies. CIO. Retrieved March
   19, 2023, from https://www.cio.com/article/409249/cios-sharpen-their-mainframe-exit-
   strategies.html
Kepes, B. (2022, January 27). IBM Sales Jump Shows the Mainframe Is Not Dead, With Hybrid
   Cloud Alive and Well. Network World. Retrieved March 19, 2023, from
   https://www.networkworld.com/article/3677548/ibm-sales-jump-shows-the-mainframe-is-
   not-dead-with-hybrid-cloud-alive-and-well.html
Mui, C. (2012, January 18). How Kodak Failed. Forbes. Retrieved March 19, 2023, from
   https://www.forbes.com/sites/chunkamui/2012/01/18/how-kodak-failed/?sh=7107e266f27a
Dignan, L. (2022, February 23). Cloud Computing Infrastructure Spending to Surge, Says IDC.
   ZDNet. Retrieved March 19, 2023, from https://www.zdnet.com/article/cloud-computing-
   infrastructure-spending-to-surge-says-idc/
Davis, H. (2011, May 31). Why Kodak Died and Fujifilm Thrived: A Tale of Two Film Companies.
   PetaPixel. Retrieved March 19, 2023, from https://petapixel.com/why-kodak-died-and-
   fujifilm-thrived-a-tale-of-two-film-companies/
Phys.org. (2011, May 31). Why Do Some Products Survive For Decades While Others Die Out
   Quickly? Phys.org. Retrieved March 19, 2023, from https://phys.org/news/2011-05-
   longer.html
Murray, D. (2022, February 25). A Few Thoughts About the Camera Market. Photography Life.
   Retrieved March 19, 2023, from https://photographylife.com/news/a-few-thoughts-about-
   the-camera-market
Statista. (n.d.). IBM's Expenditure on Research and Development Since 2005. Statista. Retrieved
   March 19, 2023, from https://www.statista.com/statistics/274821/ibms-expenditure-on-
   research-and-development-since-2005/
Statista. (n.d.). Research and Development Expenditure of Leading Internet Companies. Statista.
   Retrieved March 19, 2023, from https://www.statista.com/statistics/270854/research-and-
   development-expenditure-of-leading-internet-companies/

CHAPTER 29
Private/Permissioned Blockchains

One of the biggest challenges I have faced in the last eight years leading a blockchain business at EY is the near constant pressure to do work on private or permissioned blockchains. I have done it, but it has rarely turned out to be a good idea and so I wanted to take a chapter of this book to explain why.

Everything that you can do on a blockchain, you can do better, faster, cheaper, and easier on a centralized server. There is, fundamentally, only one reason for using a blockchain: because you need a properly decentralized system in which to execute your transactions.

Centralized server-based systems are easy to program and they scale up beautifully. Just ask the banks, airlines, and credit card companies that handle billions of transactions a day with their mainframes. Blockchains are, by contrast, very complicated. You have to copy transactional data to many different parties and then there's effectively a shared review of that data before it is confirmed. No matter how good blockchains get, they will *never* be more efficient than centralized systems.

All the things that people point to as useful for private blockchains are achievable with centralized systems at far lower costs and much faster. Distributed copies of your information? It's a standard feature of many commercial database systems. Externally verifiable timestamps that show your data has not been tampered with? Easy with hashing. Complex smart contracts? Also known as scripts. All of these and more are easier and faster on a centralized system with mature development tools.

So, if it's easier to do things on a centralized server, why bother with a decentralized system? Because decentralization is extremely valuable in and of itself. Where multiple parties need to work together without empowering a single central authority that might exploit them now or in the future, it's the only real solution that's ever been invented. That's it. That's the only reason. In a world where software and networks tend to end up as monopolies, not having your business hijacked by a powerful centralized monopoly is a very, very good reason.

Decentralization is valuable. It's also expensive. Fortunately, we live in a world where computing power and bandwidth are gradually approaching a marginal cost of zero. This is why it is possible to create blockchains in the first place. We're spending something that's nearly free – computing power – to get something that's ultimately valuable: secure, decentralized transactions.

Once you understand that the only thing a blockchain really offers that's truly unique and useful is decentralization, the idea of a centrally managed decentralized ledger starts to seem silly. I usually say stupid, but I'm always being told I need to be more diplomatic.

The Three Reasons for Private Blockchains

Private blockchains (or, as some call them, permissioned chains), exist for what I think are three main reasons. The most compelling and important one is that privacy didn't exist in any way on public blockchains in the early days. That meant that if a group of companies wanted to transact with each other all their data would be readable by anyone on-chain. In the absence of viable on-chain privacy, this was a way to achieve some privacy using blockchain technology.

The second key reason for private chains is scalability. Ethereum can handle about a million transactions a day, something that has changed only slowly over time. Before the scalability roadmap and the arrival of Layer 2 scaling solutions, companies that wanted to do lots of transactions on a blockchain had to find alternatives. Private chains can dispense with the full consensus system that exists in Ethereum and process transactions much faster, if you assume all the actors in your private network are good actors.

The third reason private chains exist is vanity (with a side helping of fear). No corporation wants to miss out on the next hot technology. Getting together with other firms and launching a consortium blockchain is a great way to capture some glory from the hot blockchain sector without taking any of the actual risk involved in embracing a new technology. A private consortium chain that contains only approved parties offers all the glory with none of the risk.

In the end, none of these turn out to be good reasons because private chains are very difficult and complex and costly to manage. Nearly all the private chains and programs that were started eventually closed down. In 2019, EY commissioned Forrester Research to get some demographic data on private chains and how they were progressing. The answers were not good and entirely predictable, but it was nonetheless great to put some hard data behind my hypothesis.

It turns out that for every one firm that's willing to join someone else's private chain, two other firms started their own. That means you'll never achieve a network effect over time. By quite a large margin, those who had actually implemented a private blockchain connection also indicated that "next time" they'd use a public blockchain.

That doesn't mean that all projects on private blockchains are useless. However, most of the time, if the project was successful on a private blockchain, then it would have been successful on a centralized server infrastructure. The return on investment was large enough to overcome the complexity and cost of a private blockchain ecosystem.

You can't get there from here

The one and only "legit" reason I've seen over the years for implementing on a private blockchain is to use that private chain as a staging area to test and develop and scale before moving to a public chain. This is a cool idea, but it comes with a very big risk: security.

When you create on a private chain, you develop and scale in an environment where everyone is very well behaved. For the same reason that corporate internal message boards are free from people hurling abuse at each other, private blockchain environments feature lots of well-behaved companies working politely with each other. On public blockchains, hackers spend their days searching your code for vulnerabilities and then exploiting them. Solutions developed and matured in these gentle private blockchain environments do not hold up well on public systems.

A more realistic approach is to come to see those public blockchain hackers not as a hassle, but as a free testing service. Instead of trying to build a fully featured solution and move it to a public chain, companies need to take a different tack and build a hardened solution slowly on a public chain. This is hard because what you can do on a public chain is limited, especially when it comes to complex business logic and privacy.

In the end, however, nearly a decade in this business has taught me that accepting the limitations of public chains, and working within them, is the only sustainable path. If you can't make it work on a public blockchain, just build a centralized system, get your ROI, and declare victory.

There's No Such Thing as Permissioned Innovation

If you have more than just a practical problem with private chains, I have a philosophical problem with them as well. Private chains have gatekeepers. People or companies that get to decide who can do what on them. And that's not good for innovation.

Never forget that the internet is a permissionless network. From radio stations to movie studios to taxi companies, many of the things we do every day started out as illegal or, at the very least, highly disruptive ideas. Streaming media? It only exists in legitimate format because the alternative was rampant piracy.

No system that has a gatekeeper will ever be fundamentally friendly to innovation because true innovation inevitably has winners and losers. The moment you create a gatekeeper, you create an entity that can be sued, prosecuted, imprisoned or just shut down. If you are an innovator, and you have to ask permission, the answer will always be "no."

SOURCES

"Seize The Day: Public Blockchain Is On The Horizon." Forrester Research, November 2019.
    https://assets.ey.com/content/dam/ey-sites/ey-com/en_gl/topics/blockchain/ey-public-
    blockchain-opportunity-snapshot.pdf.

CHAPTER 30

Proof of Work, Proof of Stake and Carbon Footprints

Blockchains, you may have heard, have an atrocious carbon footprint. This is still true for some blockchains, but is no longer the case for Ethereum.

It's worth taking a moment to explain why blockchains, including Ethereum, but especially Bitcoin, accidentally became big carbon emitters and how Ethereum departed from the norm.

When you set out to set up a decentralized transaction processing system, you suddenly encounter a number of problems that don't exist in centralized systems. One of the biggest ones is known as transaction sequencing. In a centralized system, you can process transactions on a first-come-first-served basis, and you only need to concern yourself with the timestamp of one entity in the network: the central authority. Transactions are simply queued and processed in the order they are received (or at least that's how it should be).

In decentralized systems, that's much harder. Since the foundational principle of blockchains is that each party checks the other's work, every party needs the same set of transaction data and it must be in the same order. This is a problem if everyone's transactions arrive in different orders. Instead of one time stamp to contend with, you have many, and everyone's local computer clock is slightly off. The way the internet works makes this more complicated because transactions can take different amounts of time to move around as well.

To resolve this problem, only one entity can assemble a batch (or a block) of transactions and they must distribute it to all the others. However, if that one entity is the same all the time, you don't have a decentralized system, you have a centralized one. And, if you know who it is, you could conspire with that entity to front-run transactions or prioritize your own any way you wanted. To make decentralization work, you must have a common set of data approved by a single entity for everyone to review, but the selection of that entity must be truly random.

The random selection component comes from requiring each party that proposes a block of transactions to assemble the transaction data and then solve a random number problem. There's no clever way to solve this problem. You can only solve it by trying lots of different combinations and the correct answer depends on the data in your block of transactions. The first block proposer to completely assemble a block of transactions and solve the random number problem wins and that block is adopted.

Like a game of whack-a-mole, each solution seems to create new problems that need to be solved. While Proof-of-Work (Bitcoin's consensus mechanism) is really good at ensuring a random selection of the transaction proposer, you have a couple of new problems. First, how should you compensate people for the effort that's put into this digital blockchain lottery? And secondly, what do you do if transactions seem completely out of order, or multiple parties solve the same problem with different data at the same time?

The carbon footprint problem is an unintended consequence of the solution to the first problem: compensation. In the case of Bitcoin (and earlier versions of Ethereum), the winning block proposer gets paid a few bitcoin from the network "mint." The network rules allow them to attach a couple of brand new bitcoins to the block of transactions and deposit them in their own account. This is known as "mining" and back when Bitcoin or Ethereum were worth just a few pennies each, it was a pretty harmless incentive. If you left your PC on overnight, you might come back in the morning to find you'd successfully completed a block or two and you were a couple of dollars richer.

As the price of bitcoin started to soar from pennies to dollars to thousands of dollars, the incentive to take "mining" very seriously started to emerge. Now, since there is no "clever" way to solve this problem, you just have to try lots of random number solutions. To do this, you can get a faster, more powerful computer. To do this very seriously, you can build a customized computer just for this problem. In fact, why don't you go ahead and build 10,000 custom machines and put them all in a giant warehouse next to a power plant giving you cheap electricity? As Bitcoin, and later Ethereum, became extremely valuable, the payoff from getting to mint new tokens started to get really big. In the case of Bitcoin, this peaked at a jackpot of $120,000 every 10 minutes. No surprise people were building warehouses full of energy-hungry computers to win that race.

Bitcoin and Ethereum Part Company

The consequences of this started to become obvious quickly and, starting about four years ago, Bitcoin and Ethereum parted company in their consensus mechanisms. Over on the Bitcoin side, the mining companies which had sunk billions into mining, decided that, as wasteful as this process might be, it works, and it works for them very well. As a result, the discussion and debate on the Bitcoin side of the world has focused on finding green energy sources, rather than changing the system. The Bitcoin ecosystem appears to have been largely captured by mining interests.

Over in the world of Ethereum, however, a different consensus emerged: Proof-of-Work needs to be fixed. This resulted in the development of Proof-of-Stake. The idea behind Proof-of-Stake (often referred to as PoS in the world of Ethereum) was that economic incentives could be harnessed to gain the same result as Proof-of-Work but without the duplication of effort and consequent energy wastage.

The concept behind Proof-of-Stake is that instead of assuring good behavior with random selection, you assure good behavior by having users put up a good behavior bond: a stake in the network. In the Proof-of-Stake world, block proposers put a stake in the network (a bunch of Eth) and may participate in the transaction processing work in proportion to their stake. Proposers are selected at random and if, after a block is proposed, corruption or dishonesty or incompetence is discovered, those transactions can be unwound and the proposer forfeits their stake in the network as punishment. Transaction fees are shared amongst all the staking participants.

Proof-ofStake turns out to be easy to explain and practically complex to implement. It took the Ethereum ecosystem about three years to really go from proposition to reality. A prototype Proof-of-Stake network was started and ran for a couple of years in parallel to the main network. In the fall of 2022, the two networks were merged together, an event known across the ecosystem as "The Merge." The Merge went off without a hitch and, in a s ingle leap, reduced the carbon footprint of the Ethereum blockchain by 99.5%.

Before the Merge, a single Ethereum transaction was estimated to represent about 40 KG of carbon. After the merge, about 0.04 KG for a single transaction. Bitcoin's carbon footprint, by contrast, remains largely unchanged with a very slow transition taking place towards green energy. Efforts to persuade Bitcoiners to shift to Proof-of-Stake haven't, so far, paid off, most likely because a change in approach would make their large data centers much less valuable.

The Transaction Finality Problem

The second problem created with Proof-of-Work (and not entirely fixed with Proof-of-Stake) is known as "transaction finality." As each recipient appends a block of transactions to the chain, it's possible that some recipients are headed off in a different direction or simply that your transaction wasn't included in the block. This problem gets solved as the chain gets longer and your transaction is eventually included and not at risk of being overwritten if block proposers later disagree with each other. This risk declines to zero over time, usually in a matter of minutes or hours at the most.

All of this happens automatically within the network software and, for most enterprise purposes, this doesn't matter that much. As I like to remind my clients who get scared off by the transaction finality problem, the "30" in "Net-30" is days, not milliseconds. If you're a trader, this does matter, and there are detailed solutions for advanced traders that, if not perfect, make this a manageable risk and sometimes a source of advantage. However, because those solutions get rather technical, they're beyond the scope of this book.

A Big Carbon Footprint Compared To What?

At the start of this book, I noted that in some ways blockchains are somewhat wasteful – so much redundant checking of data and transactions is involved. And while we're spending something that is cheap – computing power – to get something that is valuable – trustworthy transactional systems, cheap isn't quite the same as free and while idle computers don't have anything better to do, busy computers do consume incremental amounts of power.

As a result, it's important to understand that, even after the Merge, the carbon footprint question is not entirely solved. Blockchain transactions will always have a larger carbon footprint than a centralized system. They will also always cost more to execute.

Every Ethereum transaction ultimately gets replicated across thousands of blockchain nodes and is tested and retested by parties in the network. At the time I wrote this book, Ethereum had about 10,000 full nodes operating on the network, which means transaction data is processed 10,000 times. That has some really great advantages, such as making cheating or falsification effectively impossible. But, no matter how efficient that is, it's much more data and compute resources than are probably used in any centrally operated transaction.

As a result, I think it's important for Ethereum users to think strategically about the value that is (or isn't) created by each transaction. Replacing a simple credit card payment with an Ethereum transaction uses hundreds of times more compute power (and carbon) than the centrally-run credit card system. In most cases, I think there is little, or no, additional value created. While Ethereum transactions may, at times, be cheaper than centralized payments, that isn't a result of cost. It is most certainly a result of a lack of competition in the centralized payments business.

On the other hand, there are many cases in the enterprise world where doing a smart contract-based transaction on Ethereum is vastly more efficient than the centralized alternatives. Simple payment systems like credit cards, checks, and bank transfers, don't include any embedded business rules or logic. They can only handle very specific and simple items, like money or stocks or bonds.

Ethereum-based smart contracts can handle any kind of asset and they can include complex business logic in the process as well. Consequently, when considering the total carbon footprint of an Ethereum transaction, you need to compare it to the alternative.

For example: a typical California employee has a carbon-footprint of roughly 2 KG per working hour. If you have an employee take 30 minutes to check that supplies and contract terms match exactly in an invoice before payment is made through a centralized system, then the total "cost" for that transaction is at least 1 KG of carbon, not to mention 30 minutes of employee time as pay. By contrast, if you have a smart contract to do that automatically, you have probably used 0.04 KG of carbon on Ethereum.

Similarly, if you use tokens and smart contracts to manage your inventory and reduce your shipment by one ocean container per year, you've saved about 4,000 KG of carbon. As long as it took less than about 500,000 Ethereum transactions to get there, you've saved carbon, time, and money.

In general, my hypothesis is that wherever you have multiple parties and shared business rules and data, Ethereum results in a lower total carbon footprint as well as lower costs and cycle time.

REFERENCES

"Cambridge Bitcoin Electricity Consumption Index." University of Cambridge. Accessed March 16, 2023. https://ccaf.io/cbeci/index.

Chen, Juliet. "Is Remote Work Greener? We Calculated Buffer's Carbon Footprint to Find Out." 4/24/2020 (blog). Accessed March 16, 2023. https://buffer.com/resources/carbon-footprint/.

"CO2 Footprint per Bitcoin Transaction." *Economics Stack Exchange*. Accessed March 16, 2023. https://economics.stackexchange.com/questions/32120/co2-footprint-per-bitcoin-transaction.

"Compensation Costs in Private Industry Averaged $36.23 per Hour Worked in December 2020." US Bureau of Labor Statistics. Accessed March 16, 2023. https://www.bls.gov/opub/ted/2021/compensation-costs-in-private-industry-averaged-36-23-per-hour-worked-in-december-2020.htm.

"Ethereum Energy Consumption Index." Digiconomist, March 16, 2023. https://digiconomist.net/ethereum-energy-consumption.

Procure Desk. "Everything You Ever Wanted to Know about Purchase Order Automation." Accessed March 16, 2023. https://medium.com/@ProcureDesk/everything-you-ever-wanted-to-know-about-purchase-order-automation-2170f7ff52f4.

"Hosptial Procurement Study: Quantifying Supply Chain Costs for Distributor and Direct Orders." Health Industry Distributors Association (HIDA), May 2012. https://www.hida.org/App_Themes/Member/docs/Hospital_Procurement.pdf.

Stoll, Christian, Lena Klaasen, and Ulrich Gallersdorfer. "The Carbon Footprint of Bitcoin." *Joule* 3, no. 7 (July 19, 2019). https://www.sciencedirect.com/science/article/pii/S2542435119302557#abs0010https://spectrum.ieee.org/computing/networks/ethereum-plans-to-cut-its-absurd-energy-consumption-by-99-percent.

CHAPTER 31

Afterword

It can be really hard to understand the value of blockchain at times because everything you can do on Ethereum, you can do better, faster, and cheaper in a traditional centralized computing environment. There is only one thing that Ethereum offers that you cannot have in a centralized world: decentralization.

So I'd like to finish this book by calling back to the original question that many people have: why bother?

Decentralization is important because in the digital world we're headed towards, everything that isn't decentralized is likely to become a monopoly. Monopolies emerge when companies become more competitive, the larger they get. It used to be that this was quite difficult. As companies became larger, you needed more people, more factories, and more stores, and it became harder and harder to sustain quality and performance across such a vast scale.

Technology has, over time, kept making that easier and easier. Telecommunications and rail networks made national, and then multinational enterprises possible. The dis-economies of scale – the challenge of replicating and repeating suppliers and capacity in different areas – gets smaller if you can have one national supplier, or a national logistics network that lets you make and ship products within a region.

Digital ecosystems take this all one step further: you can have global scale instantly. Digital markets become more valuable the more buyers and sellers you have, and it becomes harder and harder to challenge the market leader. Software and networks are turning more and more products into network services that can be implemented at global scale. It's not an accident that Silicon Valley startups keep trying to turn your coffee machine or juicer into subscription services with attached digital markets.

You can laugh, but it's already worked in ways we could never have anticipated 50 years ago. As a child, taxi rides were different everywhere. In London, they were an expensive luxury. In Athens, an affordable convenience. In New York, an unavoidable expense, especially if you were going to and from the airport. They were all different and unique. Now, they're all digital marketplaces for ride-sharing.

While this is great if you're one of the companies building these networks, it's pretty bad for every other competitor in the ecosystem. Not only that, but it's also bad for consumers and workers as well because monopolies create what economists call "Deadweight losses." They don't just transfer money from one pocket to another. They reduce the total amount of wealth and consumption in an economy.

Thomas Philippon, a professor of finance at NYU, estimates that monopolies cost the average American family about $3,600 a year – or about $1 trillion dollars for the economy as a whole. And, the more we become a digital economy built on centralized systems, the faster that number will grow.

Don't misunderstand me. Ride-sharing apps are great. The uniquely special feeling of being ripped off or taken advantage of in different ways in each city was never a particularly appealing part of the taxi customer experience. Free from the "tyranny" of reputation systems and digital tracking, cab drivers could often treat you as badly as they wanted, because there was virtually no accountability in the system. Most were amazing and honest, some were not.

It doesn't have to be a choice between unaccountable fragmentation or seamless digital monopolies, however. Decentralized technologies have a wonderful track record of becoming monopolies without becoming predatory and building gargantuan industries along the way.

The internet is a perfect example. TCP/IP, the core technology that underpins all our internet communications, is free, open, and permissionless. Internet usage has literally become too cheap to meter in much of the world. Same for email, another decentralized protocol. The difference is that there's no company at the center of these networks with an obligation to maximize shareholder value. There's no inherent reason why email should be too cheap to meter, but 30% of your cab fare needs to go to pay for a software company.

To avoid a world of endless monopolies, we have three choices. We can stop the march of digitization and networks. We can regulate the heck out of all these monopolists. Or, we can build decentralized systems that can't become monopolies. The first choice isn't a real option. The second choice is a political nightmare. And the third choice is called Ethereum.

When you build your business on Ethereum and use it to digitize your operations, you are making a choice that protects your independence and contributes to our global shared prosperity. It's a good choice.

Paul Brody
San Francisco, California, U.S.A.
Sunday morning, 17 March, 2023